TABLE OF CONTENTS

Photo by Kevin Jurgens, The Garage

Left: Several Northwest rivers provide good fishing for white sturgeon. Photo by Outdoors NW

Below: Big, tackle-busting chum salmon can be found in several of Oregon and Washington's coastal rivers. Photo by Scott Cook

Above: Some of our country's best trout fishing can be found in the Pacific Northwest. Photo by Roger Carbone

Right: Perhaps the most challenging quarry Northwest anglers face is the steelhead. Turn to page 37 for information on the pursuit of this magnificent game fish. Photo by GaryLewisOutdoors.com

Freshwater FISHING
OREGON & WASHINGTON

Author
Gary Lewis

Publisher
Gary Lewis Outdoors

Editor
Merrilee Lewis

Interior Design & Layout
James Flaherty
Brian Flaherty

Print Production
Times Litho
Forest Grove, Oregon

Contributing Photographers
Gary Lewis
Brian O'Keefe
Eric Hansen
Kevin Jurgens
Robert Johansen
Rodger Carbone
Tiffany Lewis

About the Cover
Photo: "Early Spring" by Brian O'Keefe
Cover Design: Tight Line

Gary Lewis Outdoors
P.O. Box 1364
Bend, Oregon 97709
www.GaryLewisOutdoors.com

About the Author
Gary Lewis is an outdoor writer and photographer who makes his home in central Oregon. He has fished across much of the West with fly tackle, casting, and spinning gear. Born and raised in Washington, he has enjoyed fishing many of the region's most prolific waters. He is a member of the Northwest Outdoor Writers Association, and the Outdoor Writers Association of America. He is the author of *Hunting Oregon*, and *Deer Hunting*, has won awards for his newspaper columns and has written numerous magazine articles.

Foreword
When I was a year old, my dad moved our family from Seattle south to a little valley cut by southwest Washington's Kalama River and a tributary called Cedar Creek. Dad had grown up here, and my grandparents and uncles still lived on the hill, overlooking the river canyon.

Dad kept a little rowboat moored along the riverbank and, on summer evenings, would take my sister and me fishing in the long, slow stretch of river between the Pipeline and the Big Bend Hole. There were sea-run cutthroats in August, steelhead, salmon, and a few resident trout to pursue the rest of the year.

Nothing so idyllic lasts forever. When I was in second grade, we moved again, to Vancouver, Washington, where dad could be closer to his work in Portland. Fortunately, we weren't far from the fishing that I was growing to love. The Columbia River was a short walk from my back door. My mom urged me to explore along the river and the various creeks that fed it within a few miles from our home. I caught trout, perch, northern pikeminnow (they were called squawfish then), and carp. The more species of fish I caught, the more I wanted to fish.

I was with my dad when I caught my first steelhead on the North Fork of the Lewis. The next trip out, with my dad and my Uncle Jon, I caught two more. I was hooked on steelhead. In the next few years, I spent many happy hours with my uncle and my dad on the Kalama, the Lewis, the Cowlitz, and the Washougal learning more about this most spectacular of gamefish and the salmon that shared these waters with them.

Whenever we traveled, I made sure my rod and vest were packed along. In this way, I fished in and around Puget Sound, up along the Olympic Peninsula and out in the Okanogan.

At the age of nineteen, we moved again, into the foothills south of Oregon's Clackamas River and I began my love affair with Oregon's rivers and its warmwater fishing.

With friends and relatives I fished the Kilchis, the Miami, the Sandy, the Clackamas, the Nehalem and many other waters, pursuing salmon, steelhead, and anything else that would take our bait, lures, or flies.

My vision to write Freshwater Fishing - Oregon and Washington grew as I moved to central Oregon and began to fish the high lakes and freestone streams for trout. I rode horseback into the Wallowas and explored the high lakes. Still, there were fish I hadn't caught (or hadn't caught enough of). So my trips took me back to the Columbia to fill in the gaps with sturgeon, shad, and walleye. Along the way, I made trips to the Umpqua and John Day for smallmouth bass and everything else in between.

It was important for me to pro-vide a balanced perspective on what Washington and Oregon have to offer, so I have consulted with experts in both states to bring you the techniques to help you pursue the fish they are passionate about.

We examine how to catch all the species of fish that are available in both states from high lakes trout to urban carp and everything in between. The book is entertaining, but more than that it is informative, giving you everything you need to know to pursue the freshwater fish of Washington and Oregon.

The last third of the book is devoted to techniques. We will discuss fly fishing, spinner fishing, best baits, boats, fly-tying, mouth-watering recipes, how to read water, and how to bring up your children with a love for fish and the habitats that support them.

We have provided advertisers with an opportunity to tell of their products and services. You will find this invaluable in planning your adventures with information on resorts and hotels, outfitters, manufacturers, and more (see the advertiser's index on page 128). We thank the businesses that supported this book. The revenue allowed us to keep this high-quality book affordably priced.

Washington and Oregon have a wealth of fishing opportunities to challenge the angler who is willing to try something new. We have abundant warmwater opportunities in and around our most urban areas, challenging steelhead and salmon throughout most of each state, and alpine trout fisheries in the most spectacular of settings. Read this book thoroughly and enjoy freshwater fishing Oregon and Washington.

Good Fishing!

Gary A. Lewis

Gary Lewis, Author

Clockwise From Left: Don Lewis with a winter-run steelhead from Eagle Creek. Photo courtesy Don Lewis

Erik Strand with a Deschutes River steelhead. Photo courtesy Erik Strand

Sherars Falls-Deschutes River. Photo by GaryLewisOutdoors.com

The Skykomish River yielded a 17-pound first steelhead to this happy angler. Photo courtesy Hot Shot Guide Service

RAINBOW TROUT

I learned to fly fish on a freestone creek, a tributary of the Columbia, that in most places, was no wider than a sidewalk. The rainbows ranged in size from six inches to 24, depending on where you found them. Reading the water and determining likely fish-holding spots became a game that I played while I fished.

The biggest challenge was to see the fish before they saw me, to set the fly in the water without disturbing the pool.

I would psyche myself up before I reached the best hole. It was as wide as four parking places and about four feet deep. Logs and brush provided cover.

Once, I approached on my belly and looked out over the pool. A 24-inch trout fed in the narrow channel upstream. It was August and I was hoping to catch him on a hopper pattern. Keeping brush between us, I slipped over the edge and crawled down

Above: Kevin Jurgens releases a Metolius River rainbow. Photo courtesy Kevin Jurgens, The Garage

Right: Jeff Perin displays a nice Deschutes River rainbow. Photo courtesy The Fly Fisher's Place

to the dam. With just my head and shoulders above the dam, I aimed a cast upstream and set the hopper about four feet above him.

He went for it and missed. I set the hook into nothing.

Top to Bottom:
Sykes Mitchell displays a healthy rainbow. Photos courtesy Alder Creek Ranch

Sykes Mitchell with a nice rainbow from the lake at Alder Creek Ranch. Photo courtesy Alder Creek Ranch

A hatchery rainbow trout from a private pond. Photo by Gary Lewis

I leaned against the dam for five minutes, calming my nerves, resting the pool. I wanted to hook that trout. When I dared stick my head over the dam again I saw that he had moved back into position, body half-concealed beneath an over-hanging bush. It was time to try again.

His body language had changed. He was still commanding the best spot in the pool, but he seemed less secure now, having missed that big juicy grasshopper a few minutes ago. Whatever happened next, this was my last cast. I wouldn't get another chance.

My false casts measured the distance correctly, the leader turned over, straightened out, and the fly landed upstream. He drifted back, eyeing it, then thrust upward, nose emerging, engulfing the hopper. I set the hook and he was instantly out of the water, walking on his tail. There was no controlling him and I didn't expect to land him either. It was enough to have fooled him into taking the fly.

He found a submerged log, went over it, then doubled back, going underneath. Wrapped around the log, the fly pulled out of his mouth. I was left with a snag and the memory of a fish I couldn't hold.

Rainbow trout are the most available fish across the northwest. Most fishermen in Washington and Oregon learned to love fishing with a jumping rainbow on the end of their line. From southeast Oregon's desert to the rainforests of the Olympic Peninsula, the rainbow is the mainstay of northwest sport fishing. The pursuit of the rainbow, whether it is an eight year-old's eight-inch hatchery-spawned trophy, or an 18-pound Klamath Lake lunker, fires the imagination and fuels our desire to get up early on a Saturday morning when it seems the rest of the world is still asleep.

Scientists call him *salmo gairdneri*, but his more common name is rainbow taken from the pink band along his flank. In a stream environment, he may show his colors more brightly than a fish taken from a clear, cold lake. Rainbows that migrate to

Left: A brook trout from a high mountain lake. Photo by Gary Lewis

the Pacific are called steelhead when they return as adults, averaging six to 12 pounds.

Most rainbows spawn in the spring. Some spawn in the fall. They search out fast water with a gravelly bottom, running up or down lake inlets and outlets. They lay their eggs in riffles and at the tailouts of

---

When fishing smaller streams and rivers, how you approach makes the difference between having a good day on the water and catching bigger fish.

---

pools. Afterwards, they let the current sweep them downstream to sanctuary where they can regain their energy. After two months in the gravel, the eggs hatch and the fry are born.

Size varies with the environment. Mountain stream fish may average six to ten inches with a 12-incher being a true trophy. Food-rich rivers produce larger trout and still waters typically grow the largest rainbows.

In stream environments, the rainbow is a resident of fast water when he can get it. Some of the best fishing is along the seam of a riffle, where a trout can

wait in calmer water, watching the river bring his food to him.

Trout need oxygenated water, food, and shelter to survive. Learn to read the water, to find the places where these elements come together and you will soon spot the places where the biggest fish will be found.

Tackle for rainbows can be roughly divided into two categories. Adequate spinning equipment is a

Above: Big rainbow from Wickiup Reservoir. Photo courtesy Chris Shotwell

rod from six to eight feet in length with a medium action. The reel should be of good quality and equipped with four-to eight-pound test line, depending on the size of the fish encountered and the clarity of the water. When fishing for stream trout, the best lures are 1/4 to 1/8 ounce spinners, spoons, and plugs. Goodnatural baits for trout include worms, single eggs, and crayfish tails.

The bait should be presented in a manner that is consistent with how the trout are accustomed to seeing their food. Worms should drift with the current, close to undercut banks when possible. Eggs can be fished downstream of spawning trout, salmon or whitefish to good effect. Resident rainbows often gorge themselves on the spawn of other fish.

Fly equipment for most rainbow trout fishing should include an eight to nine foot rod, made to handle up to a seven-weight line. A quality reel should be stocked with at least one hundred yards of backing and a floating line. Extra spools should be kept stocked with a sinking line and intermediate lines as necessary. In most cases, the floating line will be used more often.

Rainbows feed primarily on insects in the first months of their life. As they reach the six-inch size, they began to feed on smaller fish and crustaceans, but they never lose their taste for insects. A well-stocked fly box has a good selection of patterns to match the insects the angler is most likely to encounter on the water. Caddis, mayfly, stonefly, and midge patterns in all their colors, shapes and sizes should be represented there in nymph, wet and dry stages. Leech patterns are important and so

Above: High Desert rainbow. Photo courtesy Deschutes River Lodge

are minnow patterns, so a small selection of streamers is suggested.

When fishing smaller streams and rivers, how you approach makes the difference between having a good day on the water and catching bigger fish. The idea is to spot the fish before the fish spots you.

You can get the best practice without a rod in your hand. Just go to observe. You may learn a lot more if you are not trying to catch one.

Watch for parts of the fish. A tail or a fin may catch your eye first. The trout might just look like a gray shadow against the gravel, or a hint of olive against an underwater boulder. Sometimes you can see one roll on its side, nose in the gravel. When you see a flash of silver, keep looking, you may see it again. Then go back to your car, get your rod, and tie up with a weighted nymph.

In stillwater, where I can look into the shallows, I watch for trout feeding in the weeds at the water's

edge. Often, all I see is a nose or a tail. Sometimes the fish are close enough to touch. In August and September, I'll try a hopper. Earlier in the season, I like a simple, unweighted wet fly like the brown hackle, or wooly worm.

Remember that if you can see the fish, the fish can see you. Stay out of sight if you want to catch him. Since the fish is facing upstream, you want to make your cast from downstream, behind him. Keep something between you and the fish: a bush, a tree or a boulder. Stay low. The closer you get to the fish, the lower you must be.

Can trout hear? Well, not like we do. Along a small stream or on a lakeshore, fish can feel your footsteps transmitted through the earth and water.

Walk soft, approach from downstream, and use the concealment nature has provided. You may not land the big trout, but you will have a far better chance of hooking him.

Bigger rivers sometimes intimidate the fisherman who is used to fishing smaller waters. But the fisherman who takes the time to read the water can soon find good fishing no matter how big the river. Mentally break the water up into its components and concentrate on the best section you can reach in any particular run. Determine where the fish are most

likely to be feeding then present a bait, lure, or fly to target those fish.

Sometimes you will find the best fishing close to the bank. Oregon's Deschutes River is well-known for its late May and early June stonefly and salmonfly hatches. These monster flies crawl up out of the water to dry their wings, perching in trees or in the tall grass. Sometimes, hanging out over the water, they will fall in to be swept to waiting trout.

One late-May evening stands out in my memory. A cloud of insects hung over the canyon, tan and golden-orange. Sunlight glinted on the millions of wings that the river wore like a halo.

I knotted a salmonfly imitation to the end of my line and cast upstream, letting the fly drift back to me, just two feet from the bank. A boil engulfed my fly and I missed as I set the hook too fast. That was a big fish. I cast again. The next fish took my fly and broke my line.

The fish were coming up with regularity now and my shaking hands fumbled with the knot to the sound of swirls and heavy splashes as trout took the big salmonflies and stoneflies that drifted to them on the current.

I cast upstream and along the bank, setting the fly down along the seam where the riffled water met with the smoother, slower current. The last fish had taken the fly and 12 inches of tippet when I set the hook. This time when the water boiled I raised the rod tip with a careful jab and felt the fish surge, breaking out into faster water. He was 18 inches in length and as big around as a football.

When trout are keying on a specific food source, such as insects, you will find the most fish where there is the most activity. This is a good time to match the hatch, using a fly that resembles the natural that the trout are taking. This is also a good time to try something different, like a baitfish imitation. Larger trout feed on smaller fish and smaller fish are most vulnerable when they are eating.

On a stream of any size, there are several key locations that will point you to the best fishing. Riffled water holds feeding trout in morning and evening and when clouds cover the sun. This is shallower water that moves faster than the water around it,

Above: Gary Lewis with a fat rainbow that took a crayfish pattern.
Gary Lewis photo

bringing the most food to waiting trout. Often the fish will hold at the seam, where the fast water meets the slow. Trout watch the surface for drifting morsels, darting into the current to grab a bite then resuming their feeding station once again.

Channeled, deeper water, often downstream from the riffle, holds trout throughout the day. This is sanctuary for the trout, a place to escape from winged predators.

Fishing is all about taking a break from the timetables and deadlines of everyday life

Undercut banks are another haven for trout, providing shade and concealment. This is one of the places where the feeding fish go when the sun is high.

Deeper pools hold the biggest fish, the predators that feed on smaller trout, crustaceans, and insects.

In the summer, the mouths of tributaries provide cooler water. Many trout will seek these confluences for respite from the heat.

During the spawn, in spring or fall, you may find trout in the tailouts of pools, over the spawning beds. The key to finding these trout is looking for the gravel bottom where the fish deposit their eggs. In some streams, you may not want to fish to spawning trout, but downstream you may find other rainbows feeding on the eggs that didn't make it in the gravel. Such trout can be caught on a single egg or an egg fly.

Stillwater rainbows provide different challenges. These are fish that grow larger due to the abundance

Above: A fly-caught rainbow goes back into the water. Photo courtesy Kevin Jurgens, The Garage

of food usually found in a lake. Because the food is not being brought to them on a swift current, a trout can take his time deciding whether or not to take your fly, lure, or bait. Strikes are less impulsive when a stillwater trout is the quarry.

Stillwater trout seldom hold in feeding stations like trout in a stream. Instead, they cruise, often in a circuit, watching for their next meal. Trout in a lake tend to be more opportunistic.

Left: South Twin Lake produced this opening day rainbow for Gary Lewis. Photo by GaryLewisOutdoors.com

One of the top trout destinations in the Northwest can be found in southern Oregon. It was shaping up to be the warmest day of 1998. I had never fished Klamath Lake before, but I went down to the water to look around, to see what might be seen. On purpose I had left the afternoon free in case a bit of fishing presented itself. It presented.

I sat in the bow of a flat-bottomed boat, watching a father and son casting chub and leech imitations to the edge of the tules. I was selecting a pattern of my own, ready to start fishing when my pager went off, that annoying beep-beep-buzz that kept me connected to the rest of the world.

For me, fishing is all about taking a break from the timetables and deadlines of everyday life. I apologized to my companions while I took my cell phone out of my vest and made the call. It would only happen once, I assured them. They agreed, indicating the long swim that I would be making after the next call.

The best way to leave the hustle and bustle behind is to approach the water with patience. A few clues can help you solve the riddle of catching fish on any particular day.

Weather and water conditions offer the most obvious clues. Calm weather with no wind maximizes the fish's ability to hear because of an absence of background noise. Low, clear waters tend to make the fish feel insecure as their predators have an advantage over them. Fish must remain on constant guard.

Wind, shadows, and clouds provide less than ideal conditions for furred and winged predators to get a fish dinner. It is at these times that trout may relax their defenses. The best clues, though, are under the surface, hidden from casual view.

Since fishermen attempt to fool their quarry into eating an artificial with a concealed hook, it makes sense to link an understanding of water-borne food with the proper fly and presentation.

With thousands of known patterns in existence, the important thing is to learn when to fish one fly over another. Any one of a number of items can be on the menu.

The best way to learn anything is by personal experience. Any fisherman that wants to catch more fish should keep a journal. Noting such factors as air temperature, water temperature, wind direction, lunar phase, condition of the sky and time of day can remind you, years later, why the fish were taking a particular fly over another. Or not taking flies at all.

What insects were hatching? When were the crayfish shells soft? What forage fish were present? Were whitefish or kokanee spawning?

Turning over rocks is one way to get a look at the aquatic life. Snails, caddis larvae and mayfly nymphs are often found clinging to the shelter of a lake-bottom stone.

Analysis of stomach content provides the best information about the diet of a trout. The difficulty comes in obtaining the fish in the first place. Cleaning stations at a lake can provide you with an opportunity, not to mention a few strange looks, to analyze another angler's catch.

In his book Fly Patterns for Stillwaters by Frank Amato Publications, Phillip Rowley recorded his observations of aquarium-raised aquatic insects and analysis of other trout food sources. Using a stomach pump on fish that were later released, and examining the contents of killed fish, Rowley came up with some startling statistics.

For instance, Rowley found that 50 percent of the diet of springtime trout consist of chironomids. Chironomids are two-winged flies best imitated by sparse ties on small hooks. Chironomid pupae range from under 1/8 of an inch to over one-inch in length. The adult fly is a trifle smaller than the pupae.

In the spring, forage fish account for only one percent of the stillwater trout's diet. According to Rowley, fish in less productive lakes rely heavier on smaller fish to supplement their food intake.

It may be easier to study trout than to catch them, but at some point, you need to string your rod and start casting. That hot summer day on the lake eventually yielded an 18-inch rainbow that took a weighted leech pattern. When my pager rang again, it buzzed inside my fly vest like a bee caught in a trap. No one noticed over the roar of the engine.

Leech patterns can be effective on late-season rainbows as well, as my dad and I proved one autumn day on two different waters.

Above: Brian Smith with a nice rainbow that took a Blue Fox spinner. Photo by GaryLewisOutdoors.com

A pale glow appeared in the east and suffused the cloudy sky with cold gray light. The water was still. In the wet grass, I made my way to a little bay where the summer's algae had not taken hold.

Here, tree branches hang out over the edge of the pond and thirsty roots dip fingers into the dark water. I cast my fly - a weighted and articulated purple leech - and began to retrieve.

A swirl stopped me short and I lifted my rod tip, feeling the bend that a good fish can put in my four-weight rod. He was summer-fat with broad rainbow stripes. 16 inches. I cradled him in one hand for a brief picture and let him kick away, seeking the protective cover of his hole beneath the tree.

Above: A Fall River rainbow in its fall colors. Photo by Tiffany Lewis

Some waters play out early. We left that one behind as the sun climbed higher.

The next lake was bigger and deeper, with less algae. Tall firs stood on its banks, looking over the stumps of their brothers in the dark water.

I saw trout swirling on the surface and re-tied my knot in case there were bigger fish. Casting from shore, I let the fly settle, then began the retrieve. Strip-strip-strip, pause, strip- A trout grabbed the fly and stopped it solid. Lifting the rod, I felt the weight of it and knew that this time, my 6X tippet was in for a real workout.

The fish ran and circled, then found the bottom and held it while I reeled up the loose coils at my feet. In a moment the fish was running again, straight for me. Backing up, I kept the tension on and it went by, peeling line off again. When finally it came to the bank, it took two hands to lift it for the picture, and measure against my rod. 21 inches.

When my dad invited me to fish a few of his favorite spots in the Willamette Valley, he suggested that I bring heavier leader. As I watched that fish kick away, I guessed that I had caught one of the biggest in the lake. My 6X tippet and light rod had been equal to the task. Surely there weren't any bigger fish than that. I re-tied my knot and cast again. The next fish grabbed the fly on the strip and popped it off. I cut a few inches off my tapered leader and ruefully tied on another fly.

A few minutes later, dad caught a 23-inch fish and a hook-jawed male that was even bigger. So much for my biggest fish theory.

When I smell woodsmoke in the air, see leaves skittering on the sidewalk, and catch a glimpse of fresh snow on mountain peaks, I feel a need to go and do. Trout feel the same urgency as water temperatures drop in Autumn.

Just before winter sets in, trout can often be found feeding with less caution than springtime fish as they bulk up for winter.

One of a trout's favorite foods is the leech. According to Philip Rowley in Fly Patterns for Stillwaters, this important trout food makes up 14% of a trout's autumn diet. Dragon and damsel fly larvae make up another 17%. Wooly Buggers, Seal Buggers, and other leech patterns are some of the most effective patterns in your fly box because they, by varying the retrieve, can imitate these food sources.

If you're uncertain what fly to use, try to match the color of the pattern to the shade of the water. In green water, use green or olive patterns. In black water, use black or purple. In brownish water use browns, reds, and purples.

Weight the fly at the head for the most realistic action. Leeches swim with an up and down motion, damselfly nymphs swim with a back-and-forth motion. Start with one-inch strips and vary the retrieve until you find something that works.

In a lake, the shallow water warms faster than the main body of water. Look for trout to be feeding in the shallows early in the season. As the water warms, fish will be found deeper in the lake, but still may return to the shallows to hunt their food at morning and evening.

Look at the topography of the shoreline for another indication of where to concentrate your efforts on a lake or pond. Rocky points or steep shoulders give indication that the ridge will continue below the surface. This type of structure will hold feeding rainbows in the morning and evening.

During the warmer months, one of the best places to find fish is at the mouth of an inlet stream where cooler water can be found. Such streams also carry food to waiting trout.

Underwater weed beds or woody cover such as downed trees or submerged stumps are also good bets. Such places provide cover and feed.

Among Oregon's best big rainbow waters are Crane Prairie Reservoir, Davis, Wickiup, Klamath and Agency Lakes. Top rainbow streams are the Deschutes River, Wood River and Williamson River. For large numbers of fish, look to the Crooked River east of Prineville and the Fall River south of Bend.

In Washington, some good choices for big rainbows and healthy populations include Potholes Reservoir, Medical Lake, Roosevelt Lake and Lewis County's Mineral Lake. West of Port Angeles is Lake Crescent, known for large rainbows. For stream fishing, some notably pro-

Photo by Rodger Carbone

ductive waters are the Yakima River, the upper North Fork Lewis, and the Olympic Peninsula's upper Elwha River.

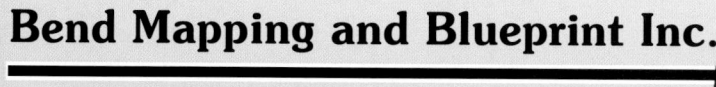
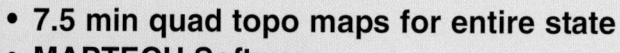

CUTTHROAT TROUT

Above: Cutthroat are strong fighters but don't jump as much as the average rainbow. Instead, they run, or thrash or dive, seeking the safety of submerged logs or overhanging willows. Photo by brianokeefephotos.com

Left: Don Lewis brings a large trout to the net. Gary Lewis Photo

Crouching on a little island in the Kalama River, I could see sea-run cutthroats stacked like firewood in the shadows of the overhanging trees. This hole was at the outside of a bend in the river and the fish sometimes stopped here to rest before moving on upstream.

"Try a black fly," Jon had said and so I knotted a No.8 black Montana Stone to the end of my nine-foot leader.

It was a 25-foot cast to the floating log and I set the fly down inches from it and tightened up the leader, watching the fly sink.

A trout rose from the depths, made one pass, turned and swallowed the fly. I waited for the line to move then lifted the rod tip into 16 inches of flashing-silver cutthroat trout.

The cutthroat trout is also known as a cutt, mountain trout, or harvest trout, if taken during the fall. It takes its name from the bright red or orange slash mark under each side of its jaw. Sea-run cutts are silver-sided and their speckles are faint while inland fish can be colorful and spotting can vary by strain.

Rainbows and cutthroats are known to inter-breed and it is possible to catch hybrids that have the appearance of a rainbow with the cutthroat slashes under the jaw.

Most sea-run cutthroat range in size from one to two pounds. Larger fish are caught however, and I have personally seen a sea-run cutthroat that would tip the scales at six pounds. Unfortunately, I couldn't hook it.

Sea-run cutthroats feed on small fish and shrimp in the ocean. Puget Sound fishermen sometimes target them in bays and around points along known migration routes. Best baits for ocean-going cutthroats include small spoons, spinners, wet flies, streamers, and shrimp.

In late spring and summer, river mouths are good bets. In August and September, the trout move up into the rivers. They feed readily in the stream and can be caught on bait, small spinners, and wet flies. They will seek out slower water than most rainbows and can be found along high banks, tucked up under shoreside brush or hiding in clean backwater beneath floating logs.

Additionally, you may find them feeding along drop-offs adjacent to the food-rich shallows. Pay close attention to submerged stumps and other structure in deep, slower-moving water.

Cutthroat are strong fighters but don't jump as much as the average rainbow. Instead, they run, or thrash or dive, seeking the safety of submerged logs or overhanging willows.

Inland cutthroats can be found in much of western Washington and in some Oregon waters. They are prolific in some high lakes and can be caught, like brook trout, on a wide variety of small lures and flies. One satisfying place to catch cutthroats is in a beaver pond. Approaching from below the dam, cast upstream to likely openings and wait for a cruising trout to grab your slow-retrieved wet fly.

The Lahontan is a rare strain of cutthroat that is found in some desert lakes. Good fishing can be found in early spring and fall for these fish.

Cutthroats don't compete well with other species. Due to their tendency to hybridize with rainbows, they are not as well represented in northwest waters as they used to be. Even where the law doesn't require you to release wild fish, care should be taken to release most, if not all of your wild cutthroat.

One of the most effective lures for cutthroat trout is a 1/8-ounce black Rooster Tail fished on four-pound test line. Seek out the slower, deeper water where the fish can rest beneath overhanging branches, secure in the shadows. Cast right to the edge of the bank or the brush, let the lure sink, twitch it and start to reel, keeping a slow retrieve yet forcing the blade to turn.

Fly anglers have good success employing wet flies and streamers in black, olive, yellow, orange, or red. In many cases, it is good to let the fly sink for a few seconds before beginning the slow retrieve. Cutthroat will take dry flies on the surface, but they are not as prone to coming to the top to eat as is a rainbow.

In Oregon, resident and sea-run cutthroat can be found in many coastal streams, including the Tillamook, Nehalem, and Nestucca Rivers. Siltcoos Lake, south of Florence, is another place where anglers can hook into cutthroat trout. For good numbers of small cutthroats, try the upper Smith River in southwest Oregon. Many smaller streams on Oregon's coast also host cutthroat trout. Consult regulations before fishing and take care to release wild fish.

In eastern Oregon, Mann Lake is one of the best places to find cutthroat trout. Best fishing is in the spring and in the fall. ODFW stocks Lahontan Cutthroat every other year in Mann Lake. Fish average 16 to 20 inches.

In Washington, cutthroat trout are found in many western waters from the Columbia system to the Puget Sound. Hood Canal and Admiralty Inlet are also good bets for saltwater fishing along the beaches. Fish Lake Washington and Lake Crescent for larger fish.

Because native cutthroat stocks are at historically low levels in some areas, wild cutthroats should be released. Read regulations before fishing.

BROWN TROUT

Left: Scott Cook cradles a nice brown trout from Wickiup Reservoir. Photo courtesy Scott Cook, Fly and Field Guide Service

There is something special about catching a brown trout. Any brown trout. Because they are among the wariest of trout and are usually outnumbered by their cousins, rainbows, cutthroats, and brook trout in northwest waters.

Browns are sometimes caught on dry flies, wets, and nymphs incidental to fishing for other species. But brown trout are predators and when specifically targeted are more often caught on streamers, spinners, and minnow-imitating plugs. Trophy fishermen, that tight-lipped fraternity whose members sometimes submit to photographs but clam up when questioned, often use flies, spoons and plugs that reach eight inches and longer. They are firm believers in the old adage that to catch a big fish you must give him something big to eat.

Most browns caught by northwest anglers weigh less than a pound, but brown trout are capable of tipping the scales at weights approaching 40 pounds. Browns are not native to North America. They were introduced on the east coast in 1883 from Scotland and German stock. Now they can be found across the continent.

An adaptable species, the brown is able to thrive in a wide variety of waters. They spawn from October through February in shallow, gravelly waters. The young are born in the spring and live an average of seven years.

Smaller fish feed chiefly on insects, freshwater shrimp, snails, and crayfish. Minnows are the primary food for browns weighing two pounds and above.

Above: Gary Lewis with an East Lake brown trout. Gary Lewis photo

Right: A big Wickiup brown trout. Photo courtesy Jon Lindsay

I caught my first brown trout in southwest Washington's Lacamas Lake when I was young, but it was a brown trout in the upper Deschutes River that stands out in my memory.

Early on a Tuesday morning, I walked upriver, looking for deeper water where I might find a decent-sized brown.

There were wisps of clouds against the pale blue morning sky. With just a half-hour before work I had to hurry. Knotting a small, sinking rainbow pattern Rapala to my six-pound test line I hooked a cast upstream.

The Deschutes makes a big sweep at that spot. A point of land pushes into it at the inside of the turn, providing shelter from the heavy current and a slow eddy. A large boulder sits about five feet from an undercut bank. A good place for a nice brown or big rainbow, I thought. Early in the morning there was still shadow from the trees on the water.

The lure splashed down upstream from the boulder and I cranked the reel, the line tightening. The surface bulged as a fish came to the top, suddenly smashing the intruder. Sweeping the rod back I set the hook solid but my line went slack as the fish ran into it.Reeling and backing up, I was able to bring the line taut again when the fish took a right turn, heading for the main river. She used her body in the fast water stripping line from the reel and I let her work against the rod, tiring in the heavy current.

Finally I gained line, bringing her to the beach, knowing she would make another run when she felt the sand on her belly. She ran again. She ran twice more and then I reached down and removed the hook from her jaw, measuring her against the handle of my spinning rod. 23 inches long.

I might have kept a lesser fish for the table and I already had fish in the freezer, so I let her slip back in. She threw water on my face with a kick from her tail.

On "fly-only" waters I am partial to forage fish patterns such as the Muddler Minnow, Kiwi Spuddler and the Matuka. Read the water. The biggest fish usually occupy the best lies. So cast to the places that will hold big fish first. These flies can work well for average size fish too. Cast across and let the current swing it into the seam of the riffle where the fast water meets slower water. Swing, swim and strip it to imitate a sculpin, caught in the fast current and heading for the shallows.

Above: Jon Lindsay with a big brown trout from Wickiup Reservoir. Photo courtesy Jon Lindsay

Whether you fish with fly or spinning tackle, your best chance at a truly big brown is in a lake.

Locate weed beds, shelves or other structure that may hold tiny trout or schools of chubs. Cruising lunkers will be keying on these locations in the hopes of picking up a little fast food.

One spring, we timed it right, hooking good-sized browns in the icy shallows of East Lake. The wind blew a heavy chop on the water and I tugged my hat down firmly on my head.

There was new four-pound test Maxima on my spinning reel and a floating Rapala dangling from the end of the rod. I cast into the wind and started to reel.

Left: An East Lake brown trout that fell for a homemade spinner. Photo by Gary Lewis

Stories I'd heard were replaying through my head. Could it really have been like they said? Would we hook brown trout as long as my arm?

I was shaken from my ponderings by a sharp tug at the end of the line. I set the hook and heard the line going from my reel. A trout came halfway out of the water and slid back in, red and black spots against his broad brown back. I backed up and reeled as the fish came at me. He was ten feet from the end of the rod when he snapped open his hooked jaw and let go of the annoying fish that had bitten him back. My rod tip straightened and I looked over at James Flaherty, seeing the smile on my face mirrored in his. Soon he had a fish on too.

Next it was Ron's turn and I dug in my spinner box for something he could cast into the wind. I pulled out one of my homemade brass spinners. A heavy No. 4 with green tape inside the blade. On his fourth cast he was into a fish and it bent his rod nearly double as he backed up toward the beach. Easily unhooked, we took a picture and let the sixteen-inch brown gently back in the water.

It wasn't long and he had another one on the beach. A hatchery rainbow this time. Between ten and 12 inches in length, it had taken the spinner farther down and so would go home with us.

We watched an osprey hunt up and down the lake, flying over our heads, searching the choppy water. It began to fly in ever-tightening circles, then stalled, wings beating against the steady wind. Folding its wings it dove, reversing just before it hit the water to slam talons into its hapless prey.

We waited to see what it would carry away but the bird stayed in the water, even going beneath the waves. After probably 15 seconds had passed, it began to shake the water from its wings and, struggling for altitude, lifted away from the water carrying what looked like a thrashing 18-inch rainbow.

The wind blew two snowstorms through and still we fished with half-inch accumulations on our hats and arms. Water froze in the guides and still we cast and retrieved, hoping for yet a bigger fish.

It was close to dark and I was heading for the propane stove and the warming cocoa when James hooked a fish. I could hear his shout above the wind and the crash of the waves on the beach. Just another fish, I thought, but looked again when I heard another shout. His rod was bent double and he was backing out of the water while the fish ran and wallowed in a vain attempt to shake the annoying steel from its jaws.

James held it against the rod to measure it as I pulled the hook free. 19 inches of brown trout slid back into the water, paused to flap its gills and pushed away, vanishing in the dark water.

The water on the cookstove was hot and we didn't waste much time stirring in the chocolate, downing our drinks as the sun's dull glow slid below the western mountains.

For just a few weeks early in the season, the big fish come out of the deeper waters to feed on the small fry. Windy mornings and evenings with heavy cloud cover give the big fish a feeling of safety from predators. This confidence makes them vulnerable to anglers who can put up with nasty weather.

Fish the downwind shallows of the big-fish lakes early in the season. Use Rapalas or similar minnow imitations in colors to match the resident baitfish. Rooster Tail spinners or streamer flies can be employed to catch big fish keying on minnows in

state record for brown trout at 27 pounds, 12 ounces. Klamath and Agency Lakes and their tributaries are home to some of Oregon's bigger browns. East of Roseburg, Lemolo Lake is another lake known to produce quality brown trout fishing.

Above: Windy mornings and evenings with heavy cloud cover give the big fish a feeling of safety from predators. This confidence makes them vulnerable to anglers who can put up with nasty weather. Photo by Chris Shotwell

Trophy fishermen, that tight-lipped fraternity whose members sometimes submit to photographs but clam up when questioned, often use flies, spoons and plugs that reach eight inches and longer. They are firm believers in the old adage that to catch a big fish you must give him something big to eat

shallow water. And do it quick, soon the waters will be warming and calming and the big browns will soon head for to the safety of deep water.

In the summer, big browns find sanctuary in the deep. Sometimes they are seen as a larger blip on the screen as kokanee fishermen bounce jigs among schools of landlocked salmon.

Browns can survive in deep water and that is where you will find the big ones when water temperatures have warmed. These big fish feed primarily on kokanee, crayfish, chubs, and other fish. Downriggers are the best way to get big lures and baits down during the heat of the day. Extremely slow trolling is very effective for fishermen targeting big browns.

When fishing deep, a braided line will add to the number of hookups. Browns have hard jaws and hard difficult to get a good hook set with stretch-prone monofilament lines. Hooked in deep water, the brown will battle the rod with twists, runs, and dives, seldom jumping. Close to the surface, the brown is more apt to jump.

On the west slope of Mount Hood, Oregon's Harriet Lake is a good bet for brown trout. Suttle, Miller, Wickiup, East and Paulina Lakes are some of the best spots in central Oregon. Paulina holds the

In southwest Washington, try Merrill Lake, a fly-fishing-only destination capable of turning out brown trout on a regular basis. Sullivan Lake in Pend Oreille County is known to occasionally produce large browns. The Colville River system is also home to German browns.

BROOK TROUT

Left: An angler prepares to release a large brook trout back into Crane Prairie Reservoir. Photo courtesy Scott Cook, Fly and Field Guide Service

Below: Gary Lewis with a brook trout from Oregon's Ice Lake high in the Wallowas.

Facing Page: Don Lewis prepares to release a nice brook trout. Photo by Gary Lewis

A September wind rattled in the yellowing cottonwood leaves and made the red and orange vine maples shiver. The last mile was a series of switchbacks that took us into Oregon's Ice Lake basin at 8000 feet above sea level.

Our guide, Barry, riding for Backcountry Outfitters, led the way on his buckskin, a pack-horse on a lead rope behind him. I was mounted on a bay and Dad brought up the rear on a sure-footed gray.

We rode with the anticipation of hooking into a few of the alpine brook trout for which the Wallowa Wilderness is well-known.

The brook trout, also called squaretail, speckled trout, and eastern brookie, is classified as a char. An easy way to tell the difference between a trout and a char is by looking at the spots. A trout has dark spots on a light background. A char has light spots on a dark background.

The brookie is one of the most beautiful of the trout/char family. Its back and sides are bluish- or brownish-olive with light yellow or pink spots, sometimes surrounded by a light blue halo. Its flanks are rosy-orange and similarly speckled. The darkish fins are accented by a white pinstripe on the leading edge. Its meat is also colorful, usually a brilliant orange.

I thought about the first brookie I ever saw. I was fishing a private lowland lake in western Washington, throwing a black Rooster Tail spinner, when my rod bent over. Used to catching rainbows here, I was surprised to finally reel in a 14-inch brook trout.

I could see the lake through the trees, deep blue and green. Alpine meadows with weather-twisted firs and pine trees gave way to steep, landslide country where little in the way of plant life grew. High above, were granite cliffs and rocky, rugged peaks. I shaded my eyes with my hand to look. Somewhere up there, I was told, there were mountain goats.

Barry turned his horse left and we crossed Adams Creek, leaning forward in our saddles as the horses scrambled up the high bank. We rounded a knob and followed a narrow trail along the rocky beach.

At the water's edge, we saw brook trout, our reason for being here. A few eight to ten inch brookies hung suspended in the clear blue water where the shallows gave way to deeper water.

We made camp in a little basin away from the water, moving a few rocks to make room for the tent. While Dad opened our packs, Barry borrowed a fly rod and headed down to the water. I was right behind him.

Before I could even make a cast, Barry had hooked and landed a ten inch brook trout. It took three casts before I hooked a fish. I was using a No. 14 Adams and I set it down outside of the shallows and saw a brook trout, coming up and up from the dark green depths. He opened his mouth and took the fly back down. It promised to be a good day of fishing.

Barry soon retired for a nap and a lunch of trout while Dad and I continued on around the lake. We moved down the beach a few yards whenever the bite slowed.

It didn't seem to matter what fly we used. After I lost the Adams I switched to a bead head Prince Nymph. We caught fish on whatever fly we tried. A Mosquito pattern worked as did the Hare's Ear and Zug Bug. Streamer patterns caught fish and so did a Mouserat that I cast alongside a log and swam back.

The most fun were the grasshopper patterns though. My favorite was a low-profile pattern with a calf tail wing and the hackle tied in parachute fashion. We would cast these along the shoreline or just outside of the shallows to entice cruising fish. These fish knew how to eat a grasshopper. They exploded on top of the fly, seeming to want to dunk the hopper before swallowing it. In the clear calm water we could often see the fish as it climbed to smash the fly.

It was three o'clock when we finally stopped for lunch, carrying five brookies back to camp and frying them over a small fire.

Afternoon gave way to evening and Dad and I fished until it was nearly dark. The trout were so hungry that I truly believe I could have caught 150

fish that day if I had kept at it. They ranged in size from six to 11 inches with most of the fish measuring between eight and ten inches.

Each fish was different in appearance though all were brookies. Some had dull coloration while others were brilliantly colored with orange fins tipped in white. Some had extremely large heads with underfed bodies. These were older fish whose bodies had not kept up with the growth of their heads. Too many fish and not enough food.

In the morning the fish didn't come as quickly to the fly as they had the previous night. I guess I spent more time looking at the mountains and the wildflowers too, hoping to imprint on my mind what I was seeing.

In the afternoon, we rode out, leaning back in our saddles as the horses picked their way down the switchbacks. Looking down I noticed that my horse liked to walk the ragged edge where the trail ended and thin air started. Often there was nothing below my stirrup, but a long tumble to the jagged rocks below.

I would ride this trail again, with a fly box restocked with grasshopper patterns and small dry flies. Pure mountain air, good fishing, clear sky, creaking saddle leather and the easy gait of a good horse. What better way to spend a few summer days?

For Oregon's brook trout, try Timothy Lake on Mount Hood, Crane Prairie Reservoir or the Upper Deschutes River, or any one of a number of alpine lakes in the Wallowa Wilderness.

Brook trout in Washington can be found in many alpine lakes, streams, and beaver ponds.

Top: Jeff Perin displays a handsome brook trout from Little Lava Lake. Photo courtesy Jeff Perin, The Fly Fisher's Place

Facing Page: While fishing with Backcountry Outfitters, Gary Lewis tries trolling for brookies from atop an unwilling horse. Photo by Gary Lewis

Left: A brook trout from Crane Prairie Reservoir. Photo by Scott Cook, Fly and Field Guide Service

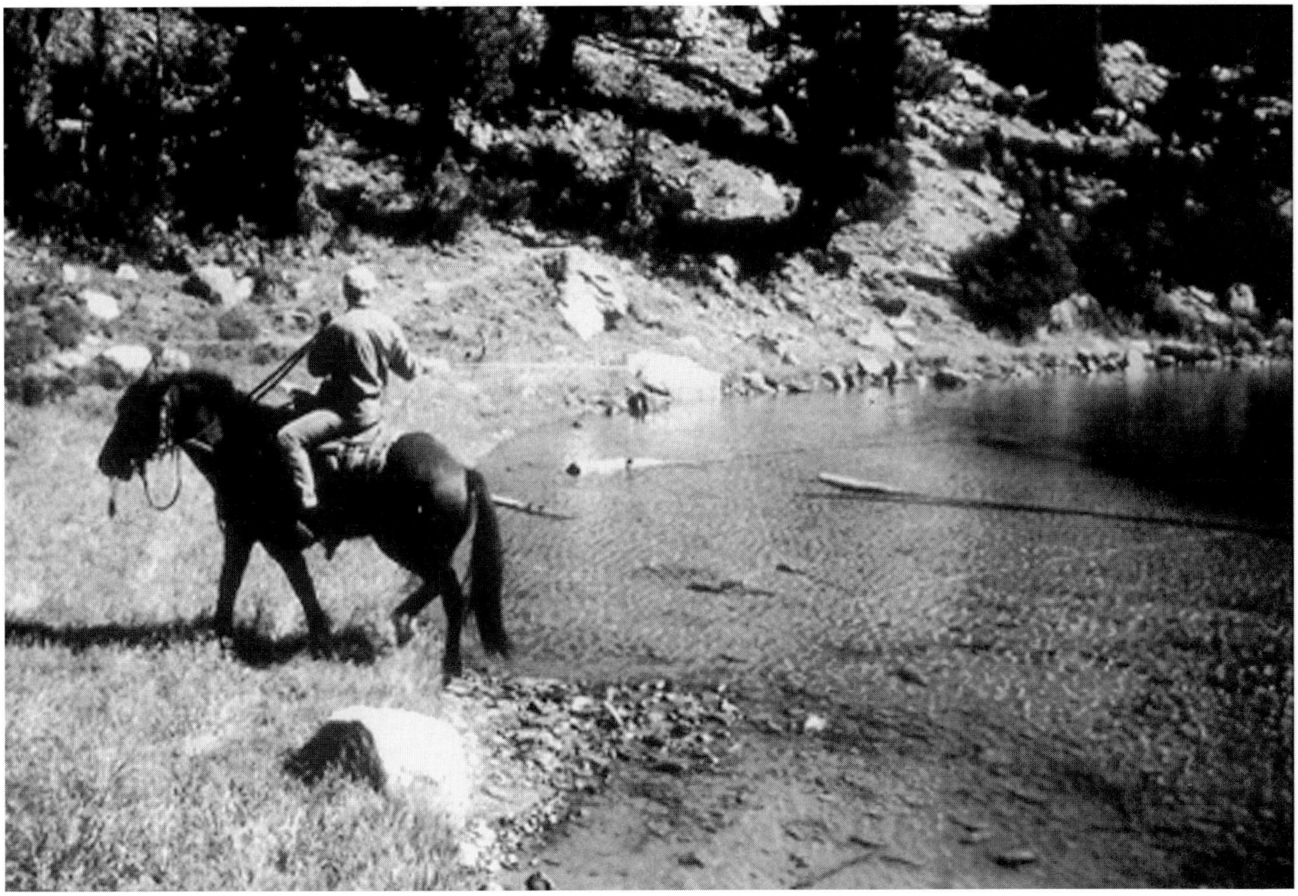

LAKE TROUT

Lake trout, also called mackinaw are, in fact, char. But whatever you call them, they are creatures of the deep-water lakes. Since their preferred temperature range is from 48 to 52 degrees, they are commonly found in depths of 50 to 150 feet. In the spring, however, and in late fall and winter, when temperatures near the surface cool, big lakers can be caught in shallow water.

The big char feed primarily on fish. In many lakes, kokanee are the preferred food, but other species such as chubs, whitefish, squawfish, rainbows, cutthroats and bull trout might be on the menu.

Lake trout may be found at different depths during the course of a day. Some fish will be chasing kokanee, slashing through a ball of bait at 80 feet, feeding until they are full, then dropping down to the 100 to 150 foot depth to rest and digest their food. They compensate for changes in water pressure by burping air through a duct connecting their swim bladder to their esophagus.

They are slow-growing fish. In most waters it takes ten or eleven years to grow a five-pound fish. Lake trout can live as long as 40 years. The largest lake trout on record was caught with a net in Saskatchewan's Lake Athabasca. The fish weighed 102 pounds.

Above: Gary Lewis with a 14-pounder from Odell Lake. Big lake trout feed on kokanee, chubs, whitefish, squawfish and other smaller fish. Gary Lewis photo

Oregon's Odell Lake is famous for its lake trout

When fishing for lake trout, medium to medium-heavy spinning or baitcasting gear works best. Use eight to 15 pound test line unless targeting extremely large fish. This is a great time to use braided line because it does not stretch and deepwater bites are felt, and responded to, faster.

Oregon's Odell Lake is famous for its lake trout. And well it should be. Odell's lake trout fishery was established by stocking efforts in the early 1900's. The state record lake trout was caught in Odell in 1984, a trophy that broke the 40-pound barrier. The Oregon Department of Fish and Wildlife has recorded lake trout, also known as mackinaw, in the 50-pound range. Anglers from all over the Northwest come to Odell in the hopes of boating one.

I had brought my daughter Jennifer, and we were hoping that she would get a chance to do battle with one of the lake's larger citizens.

We fished with Dana Knepper of Central Oregon Spinnerbaits from Crescent Lake. His boat is an eighteen-foot Starcraft, equipped with a 90 hp Mercury outboard. He has two Cannon downriggers, sporting ten-pound weights to take our baits to the bottom. We would use 7'-6" trolling rods, rigged with casting reels and 25-pound test line.

Dana favors an M-2 Flatfish in a coho pattern, baited with two whole nightcrawlers, trailing off the rear treble. He rigged both rods the same way, lining up the Flatfish behind a series of flashers. The downriggers took them to the bottom and we were underway.

We started fishing in 140 feet of water, trolling at low speed. From time to time, Dana would "ring the dinner bell," by dropping the downrigger into the mud, then cranking it back up again. The theory is that the lake trout are sometimes intrigued by the sudden stirring in

the mud, they swim over to investigate and spot the Flatfish moving away, then they strike.

Dana changed directions often, keeping a sharp watch on the depth finder. When the screen indicated a depth change, he would raise or lower the weight as needed to keep the lures from five to ten feet off the bottom. He tried speed changes and zigzagging to spark the bite. Nothing seemed to work. Such is

fishing. Finally we changed locations, running the boat east to work another section of the lake.

In the summer, lake trout are deepwater fish. Dana fishes Odell and Crescent and finds macks between 140 to 160 feet down through July and August. The fish will move up and down in the water column on a daily basis, feeding on kokanee. But during the summer, you need to go deep to find them.

In Odell, there is a one mackinaw a day limit. To be kept, fish must be thirty inches in length. It was two minutes after noon when we had the first hit. Dana had just changed the depth on the bait when Jennifer's rod bent over. To date, her best trout had been a twenty-inch rainbow from Crane Prairie Reservoir. By the bend in the rod, it was evident that this fish was much bigger. The muscles in her nine-year old arms were straining. I showed her how to lift and reel down, then lift again, gaining line on the fish.

After about eight minutes, she had the big fish close to the surface. Dana stabbed for it with the net and brought in a 35-inch laker that later weighed in at almost 15 pounds. The quiet little girl, with more patience than most

Above: Dana Knepper with a big lake trout from Odell Lake. Photo courtesy Dana Knepper

Right: Dana Knepper readies the net for another big mackinaw. Photo by Gary Lewis

Right: A downrigger is important for reaching lake trout and kokanee in deep water. Photo by Gary Lewis

Below: Oops!. Photo by Gary Lewis

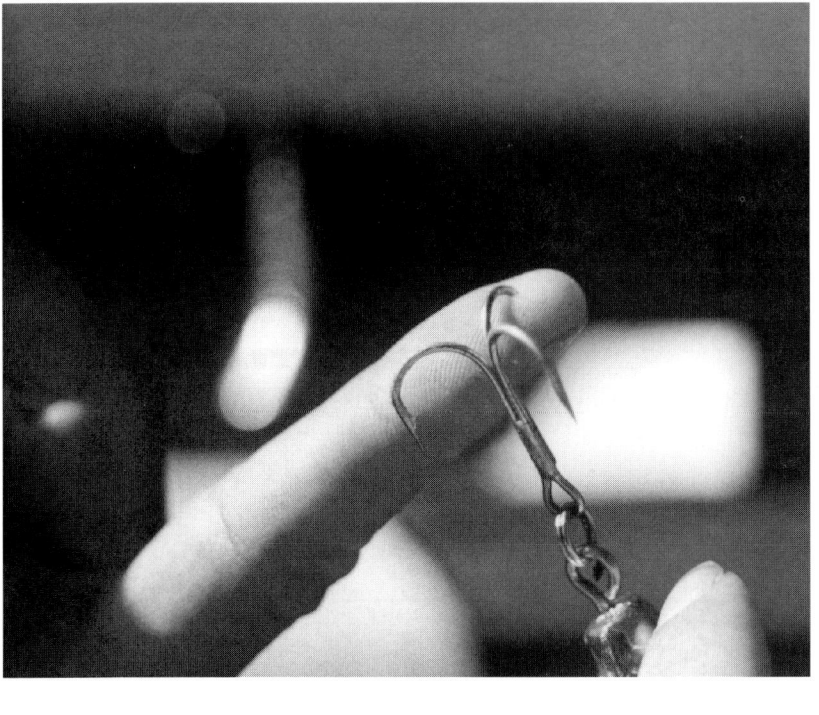

In the summer, when fish are deep, you can reach them with down-riggers for precise depth control. Another method to reach deep-water lakers is trolling a three-way rig. Tie a three-way swivel to your mainline and tie a three-ounce weight to a four-inch dropper from your swivel. Use a Sutton Spoon, a Rebel Minnow, Rapala or other fish-imitating lure tied to two feet of leader. Lower the rig carefully to keep it from tangling before you start trolling.

When lakers are feeding on schooled kokanee, you can entice them by jigging spoons. After you locate fish on the depth finder, do a vertical jig with a one or two-ounce lead-head jig or spoon. Lift the lure with long sweeps of the rod, keeping your line tight while the lure sinks.

anglers, was elated. She was also done fishing for the day. We wanted to be off the water by one o'clock. Time was ticking away on my chances of boating a big one.

We were reeling in, ready to head back to the dock when it happened. Again, the sudden change in direction sparked the bite. He fought with short surging runs and head-shakes, but soon we could see him behind the boat. Dana leaned in with the net and scooped him up. He was big and deep in the body, but not as long as Jennifer's. The tape told the tale. Her fish was an inch longer.

When you find them in shallow water, cast or long-line troll spoons and plugs.

Fortunately, there are many lakes in the Northwest where good lake trout fishing can be found. In Washington, try Lake Chelan, Loon Lake, Lake Cle Elum, Bead Lake, Bonaparte Lake, Kachess Lake and Deep Lake in the Okanagon. Other good bets are Northeast Washington's Horseshoe Lake and Deer Lake. Try Odell Lake and Crescent Lake in Oregon.

ATLANTIC SALMON

Atlantic salmon were introduced to the Pacific Northwest to provide fishermen with new angling opportunities. In the 1960s fisheries managers in Oregon and Washington began to stock Atlantics in several mountain lakes in each state.

As outlined in Foghorn Outdoors' excellent publication *Washington Fishing* by Terry Rudnick, commercial fish farmers in the Puget Sound have lost large numbers of Atlantic salmon in recent years. These escapees sometimes show up in the nets of salmon fishermen in both salt and freshwater in the Puget Sound system. It appears that Atlantic salmon haven't established runs in any rivers at this point.

The Atlantic salmon has a square tail and a long body with dark fins and tail. The top of his head and back are blue-green going to silver on the flanks and white on the belly. Black markings and glimmers of pink and blue are on his head and back. Landlocked Atlantic salmon grow to 20 inches and beyond.

The best bets for catching Atlantics in the Pacific system are East Lake and Hosmer Lake in central Oregon. Any method that will catch rainbows or browns in East Lake is likely to spark the interest of an Atlantic salmon. Spoons, spinners, plugs and bait will all catch Atlantic salmon. Early in the season, when the wind blows a chop on the surface of the lake, you can catch Atlantics (and browns and rainbows) close to shore with any baitfish imitation.

Later in the year, when the sun shines on the water and the lake reflects the pines like a mirror, the fish will be deeper. Get up early in the morning to catch Atlantics close to shore. Target weedbeds and flats until the sun and ospreys chase the fish to deeper water. In the afternoon, if there is no insect hatch in progress, fish close to the weedbeds or along the rockslide.

To catch fish in this shallow, clear water, you need to make long casts with long, light leaders

---

Use a slow-sinking line and ten feet of leader tapered to a four-pound tippet. Any streamer that imitates a small rainbow, or tui chub will catch fish. Sweep the rod left or right and turn the boat frequently to mimic the evasive action of a small fish. Such tactics provoke strikes from predatory fish.

In Hosmer Lake anglers are restricted to fly-fishing tackle with barbless hooks. Both brook trout and Atlantics are available. Atlantic salmon must be released. Fish feed on mayflies (Callibaetis), damselflies, dragonflies, water boatmen, leeches, chironomids, and crayfish. To catch fish in this shallow, clear water, you need to make long casts with long, light leaders.

Some good patterns for fishing Hosmer Lake are the Troth Pheasant Tail, Baetis Soft Hackle, Parachute Adams, White Woolly Bugger, Palomino Midge, Griffith's Gnat, Stalcup Adult Damsel, Gray Ghost, and Mickey Finn.

Both Hosmer and East Lake are high mountain lakes. Some years the roads may be blocked by snow on the trout season opener. Before traveling a long distance, make a call to a local fly shop to get a preview of the road conditions.

Above: Angler at Hosmer Lake...
Photo by Kevin Jurgens, The Garage

BULL TROUT

Left: Jennifer Phelps with a bull trout she caught in the Metolius River in central Oregon. Photo courtesy Justin Karnopp, Central Oregon Outdoors

Below: Brett Dennis displays a big bull trout from Lake Billy Chinook. Photo courtesy Brett Dennis

It was June and I was fishing the Metolius River at mid-day. I had caught a couple of smaller trout upstream but was hoping to hook something bigger now. I worked out thirty feet of line and cast across the riffle, letting the current catch the fly line and sweep my streamer across and down.

At the end of the swing I started to bring the fly back with short, sharp strips. The water bulged behind my imitation and I kept it coming as a great shape rushed it. At least fifteen-pounds, the big char turned away in four inches of water. I guessed I had missed my chance but he chased it again on the next cast, bumping the streamer with his nose this time.

Bull trout are slow-growing, reaching maturity in about five years. They may live for twelve or more years, reaching 30 pounds in size in waters where food is abundant. The average reproduction cycle is every other year.

The bull trout is a colorful fish. His back and flanks are olive or brown, sprinkled with red, orange, pink or yellow spots. His belly is white and his tail forks slightly. His head is long and broad.

It should be no secret to anglers that bull trout are in trouble across much of their

Bull Trout and Dolly Varden are very similar in appearance, but have some differences in internal structure. Bull trout grow larger on the average, and tend to have a longer, broader head. In addition, Dolly habitat tends to be coastal, while bull trout inhabit inland waters. Dollies are more apt to spend some time in the ocean than bull trout. In a few northern rivers, both species can be caught in the same water.

range. Populations in Oregon's Metolius River system are in good shape, but elsewhere numbers have dwindled. One of the reasons is because of the introduction

Just before winter sets in, trout can often be found feeding with less caution than springtime fish as they bulk up for winter.

of eastern brook trout, another char. When the two species mingle, the offspring is sterile. Brook trout reproduce earlier and are more prolific, slowly replacing bull trout. In recent years, the Oregon Department of Fish and Wildlife has encouraged the retention of brookies to reduce this effect.

In the Metolius River, angling is restricted to fly tackle only. Anglers use 6, 7, and 8-weight rods equipped with hi-density sink-tips and weighted streamers. Flies that imitate large trout, kokanee, or, in late fall, decaying kokanee flesh, are your best bets. When kokanee fry are running downstream, small streamers that imitate them are effective.

In the lakes where bull trout angling is permitted, large minnow imitations are extremely productive, especially early in the season. Anglers troll plugs behind the boat or cast to structure. Bring a variety of minnow imitating plugs and soft swim baits. Don't be afraid to use large baits.

For your best opportunities at catching bull trout in Oregon, fish the Metolius River, Laurance Lake, Lake Simtustus, and Lake Billy Chinook. In Washington, Lake Chelan harbors a population of bull trout. Because fisheries managers are paying close attention to bull trout populations, check regulations before angling for bull trout.

Above: Justin Karnopp, tied into a trout on the Metolius River. Photo courtesy Justin Karnopp, Central Oregon Outdoors.

DOLLY VARDEN

The Dolly Varden, a char, was named for a colorful character from a Charles Dickens novel. It has a white belly, a slightly forked tail, and brownish or greenish flanks stippled with orange, pink, and red spots. Where food is abundant, they can grow fat and long. It is a predator that, after it reaches about ten inches long, begins to feed heavily on smaller fish. One to three pounds is the average size, but Dolly Varden in excess of five pounds are not uncommon.

Dolly Varden spawn in the fall. Some fish migrate to saltwater while others stay in their native streams all their life. The Dolly's range extends as far south as Washington's Puget Sound.

Fish for dollies with lures and flies that appeal to their predatory nature. Spinners, such as the Rooster Tail, Mepps, Metric and Blue Fox are effective on dollies. They will also take small spoons in black, silver, nickel, brass or copper finish. Egg flies are productive for Dolly Varden during the seasons when other species are spawning. Bunny Leech and Flesh Fly patterns such as are used for bull trout will also work for Dolly Varden. The top flies, though, for taking big dollies are those that imitate baitfish. Some good choices are the Black Nose Dace, Mickey Finn, Muddler Minnow, and Zonker.

Where legal, salmon egg clusters, or a nightcrawler with a bit of chartreuse yarn can also tempt dollies.

For Dolly Varden in Washington, ply the rivers of the Puget Sound and the Olympic Peninsula. Check the regulations before fishing for Dolly Varden.

Top: Parachute Royal Coachman   **Above:** This 19-inch Dolly Varden took a Teeny Nymph. Photos by Gary Lewis

KOKANEE

We cut the engine in 50 feet of water off a rocky point. There was a light breeze that would blow us toward the north shore. Paying out line, I dropped my jig, letting it tumble and fall. Far off in the distance, lightning flashed. We counted to hear the thunder and calculated the distance. Seven miles.

My jig struck bottom and I cranked it up a few feet and let it bounce, imagining the kokanee below, watching my jig, turning away, then following it again.

Lighting flashed again and thunder rolled. Was it closer this time?

"Got one." It was Jeff with the triumphant grin and the pulsing rod. He played the fish up to the boat and Scott slid the net under it. Then it was my turn as my rod bent and danced with the fish beneath us. The fish came fast for a few minutes, sometimes following the jig all the way to the surface.

I reeled in to change lures and, while my line was unencumbered, it lifted off the water, in defiance of gravity, suspended in the air. Electricity arced from my graphite rod to the aluminum tube of the boat canopy.

"Hey," someone said, "my hair's standing on end."

Lightning crackled across the sky. I broke my rod down and we pointed the boat toward shore, praying that we could make it out of the water before a bolt from heaven made this our last fishing trip. My two kokanee would have to be enough for this night. An awesome light show with thunderous accompaniment, lit up the snow-capped peaks until midnight.

Photo courtesy Dana Knepper

Most summer kokanee trips aren't cut short by weather. More often it is a surfeit of fish that ends the day. Many Oregon and Washington lakes have enough kokanee to justify the large limits. When you want to catch a lot of fish, when you need to stock up on good-tasting meat, kokanee fishing might be the answer.

Kokanee are the landlocked sockeye salmon that don't grow as large as their ocean-going cousins do. Full-grown, they average twelve to eighteen inches. In lakes where kokanee are abundant, they may not grow as large due to the competition for food. Silver-sided, males turn red at spawning time while females turn gray or dark green. In September, sexually mature fish seek out inlet streams for spawning. Good fishing can be found in early September, where kokanee congregate waiting for rain to swell the streams, making upstream passage easier.

Most fishermen seek them out in spring and summer when the fish are healthy and well-fed. Kokanee travel and feed in schools of similar-sized fish and can be easy to catch when conditions are right. They feed on a diet of insects, crustaceans, plankton, midges, and minnows.

The two most popular ways to fish for kokanee in the Northwest are trolling and jigging.

According to fishing tackle designer Dana Knepper, jigging is the most effective technique in the springtime on many waters. As the surface water warms, bigger fish will seek out deeper water.

The Buzz Bomb is one example of the types of jigs employed for kokanee. Common sizes are 3/4 ounce and one-ounce models. These jigs are made from lead or brass bodies and painted in different fish-catching colors. Fluorescent orange is one of the most popular finishes.

Above: When trolling for kokanee, make frequent changes in lure direction, speed, and depth. Paulina Lake yielded this kokanee and several more.

Knepper prefers the brass body of his own design, the Hexagon Hooker. He believes that the brass is key to catching more kokanee. Fishing the jig close to the bottom, the lure will tick on rocks. The ring of the brass striking stone gives a higher-pitched tone than a lead jig will produce, and this, Knepper asserts, is more attractive to kokanee.

When fishing a jig for kokanee, the aim is to imitate a crippled baitfish. Often, the kokanee will be feeding close to the bottom. Drop the lure to the bottom, crank it up a few inches, then raise the rod tip 12 inches and let the jig flutter back down.

Lure action is very important. To achieve the optimum control, use a six to seven-foot medium action steelhead rod, and a level wind bait-casting reel equipped with six-pound line.

Many anglers switch to trolling for kokanee in early summer. The larger fish will be found in deeper water. A three-ounce "banana" sinker can be used to take your bait down to about 40 feet. Lead-core line is another option for serious kokanee trollers. A small Herring Dodger or Ford Fender should be used, followed by a leader of twelve to 24 inches and the terminal tackle. At the end of the leader, you can use a No. 6 or 8 hook baited with white corn or a lure like a pink Rooster Tail or one of the specialized kokanee lures like the Kok-A-Trolla or Crescent Fluorescent manufactured by Central Oregon Spinnerbaits.

At the depths where kokanee are sometimes found, fluorescent and glow-in-the-dark paint schemes can make the difference between catching a few fish and "limiting-out." It can be dark down there, especially when the sun is not directly on the water.

Trolling and jigging will continue to take good catches of kokanee up until the fish begin their spawning runs in early September.

When trolling for kokanee, make frequent changes in lure direction, speed, and depth. Sometimes the change in direction will spark a bite from an otherwise uninterested fish.

There is ample opportunity to catch kokanee in Oregon and Washington lakes. Some of Oregon's best waters include Paulina Lake, Suttle Lake, Lake Billy Chinook, Crescent Lake, Odell Lake, Green Peter Reservoir, Wallowa Lake, Timothy Lake and Detroit Lake.

In Washington, kokanee can be found in more than 60 lakes and reservoirs, including Yale Lake, Lake Merwin, Upper Lake Roosevelt, Lake Chelan, Potholes Reservoir, Lake Wenatchee, Conconully Reservoir, and of course, Kokanee Lake.

JACK NICKLAUS. TOM FAZIO.
THEY WROTE THE BOOK ON GOLF COURSE DESIGN.

NOW THEY'RE ADDING A NEW CHAPTER IN BEND, OREGON.

Central, Oregon, with its abundance of world-class outdoor activities and 300 days of sunshine annually, has been described as adventurous, exciting, even inspiring. And now that Pronghorn is being added to its landscape, you can add, "luxurious." Ownership and membership at Pronghorn will allow you to enjoy an unparalleled lifestyle in this magnificent setting along with Oregon's first Jack Nicklaus Signature Golf Course, Oregon's first Tom Fazio Championship Golf Course and a world-class private club & spa. All nestled comfortably within 20,000 acres of protected BLM land. To learn about our newest phase of homesites and villas, which start at $350,000, call 1-800-541-9424.

PRONGHORN™

Central Oregon's Premier Golf Community

DISCOVERY CENTER
830 NW Wall St. • Bend, Oregon 97701

1-800-541-9424
www.pronghornclub.com

Marketed by Pronghorn Properties

Terrestrials: A Fable for Fly-Rodders

Once upon a time there was a Grasshopper. *All summer he played and sang and lazed about in the long grass at the edge of the river. His neighbor, the Ant, was busy storing away grain for the coming winter.*

Summer was good to the grasshopper. He had grown big and fat on the bounty that grew around him and only had to move fast whenever a heavy-footed fisherman walked by.

The Ant worked hard, carrying grain back to his family. Sometimes he would talk to the Grasshopper as he passed. "Friend, while it is warm you should gather food for the cold months ahead."

The Grasshopper would laugh and answer, "Neighbor, you should relax and sit by the river with me and enjoy life while the weather is nice."

So one day the Ant set down his burden and went with the Grasshopper to the edge of the river. They climbed a blade of grass. The Ant looked across, enjoying for a moment the scenery and the companionship, relaxing a little. He didn't say anything to the Grasshopper but he thought to himself that maybe the Grasshopper was right, maybe it was okay to enjoy life instead of working all the time.

A light breeze rustled the grass and then a gust of wind blew both the Grasshopper and the Ant into the river. A great fish with a brilliant rainbow stripe and black spots on its back, lifted its head out of the water and ate the Grasshopper. A moment later it ate the Ant.

There are two morals to draw from this story. The moral for fly fishermen is that trout will eat insects blown from the land. These are called terrestrials.

Some portion of a trout's diet is made up of land-borne creatures. Besides ants and grasshoppers, fish will feed readily on bees, moths, beetles, crickets and inchworms.

Once I was fishing for steelhead with a friend of mine. On this particular day we were having trouble enticing one of the big fish, though we could see them well enough in the clear water.

My friend tied on a No. 12 Bumblebee pattern and crawled out on the log jam, keeping his head low so as not to spook the fish just downstream.

I watched him fooling around, not saying anything. He was always ready to try something different. There he goes, I thought, trying something strange again, wasting his time.

He lifted the tip of his rod over the top of the log and let the fly drop to the smooth water downstream. That little bee triggered something in the brain of a big fish. The surface exploded as a steelhead detonated on that little fly.

Once I fished a little pond on a mountain stream. It was a hot afternoon but half of the pond was in shadow and fish were rising in the shade.

I threw some grasshoppers in - big slow ones that couldn't escape from this heavy-footed fisherman and noticed that most of the fish were too small to eat the insect all in one bite. I wouldn't be able to hook too many fish on the large hopper patterns I was carrying in my box. I tied on a No. 14 Black Ant pattern and cast along the shore. The trout weren't big but they were hungry and there were a lot of them. The biggest trout measured nine inches.

In my boxes are several summertime standbys I might try when the fish aren't taking aquatic patterns. My favorite is the grasshopper. Let the current carry it along a grassy bank to waiting trout. A cricket pattern works on the same principle.

Another favorite pattern is the deer hair mouse. Cast it toward the bank and swim it slowly across the surface.

For those instances when I am fishing for bluegill with dry flies, I like to have a beetle pattern to fall back on. I carry an inchworm pattern as well. Of course, I always have a good selection of those hard-working black ants.

Finally, the second moral to our story is as important as the first. It is for those of you who work all the time and have never taken a moment to go sit by the river to relax and look. Don't go there. It's not safe. There are big fish there. They may eat you.

STEELHEAD

Above: Greg Cobb with a Deschutes River steelhead. Greg used his spey rod to land this big native fish. Photo by www.theflyboxoutfitters.com

It was June 27, 1981. A gentle wind stirred the tops of the trees and a blacktail deer stepped out of the island brush to get her evening drink.

I knotted a Stee-Lee to my line and checked the knot to make sure it wouldn't slip. Here, the speed of the river was about that of a fast walk, probably six feet deep. If I cast as far as I could, I might be able to hit the sandbar on the island.

Next to the sandbar was a deep trough. My lure splashed down a little upstream of the sandbar and I let it sink and tightened up on the line, allowing the spoon to work through the slot before beginning to reel.

Something stopped it and I set the hook. Whatever it was, it was coming at me. It kicked, turned and ran. I reeled when it gave me line, let it run when it took line. "Fish on," I yelled to Dad. In a few minutes it was over. The North Fork Lewis River yielded my first steelhead - a nine-pound female. Not the first I ever hooked. But the first I landed after two years of trying.

Steelhead are like that. You have to earn them. The first one seldom comes easy. If it does, watch out, because you will have to earn your steelhead later.

That's why we chase them I guess, because we have to work so hard to figure them out at first.

And once we think we've got them figured out, we try a different river and find that we can never know enough about steelhead.

Many anglers fish for years before they land their first one. In fact, plenty of Northwest fishermen have never landed a steelhead, nor even hooked one. Is it because there is something difficult about catching a steelhead? Well, maybe. To consistently catch steelhead doesn't require extraordinary fishing skill, it demands a knowledge of the water, and of a steelhead's life.

He is a sea-run rainbow trout. Programmed to run downstream to the ocean, to roam far and wide at sea, growing fat on the bounty he finds in saltwater. To survive, he must stay out of gill nets and outrun birds, seals, sharks, salmon and other predators. In a year, or two or three, a biological impulse triggers his return to freshwater and he seeks out the stream of his birth, to spend a few months in freshwater before spawning.

It is a journey of anywhere from a few miles through tidewater to hundreds of miles of river, fish ladders, rapids and waterfalls. He runs a gaunt-

Left: There's nothing mystical about enticing a steelhead to bite, but there is magic in what happens after you set the hook. Gary Lewis Photo

Below: Lisa Vlessis caught her first steelhead ten minutes into her first steelhead trip. Photo courtesy The Patient Angler

let of seals, commercial and tribal fishermen, sport fishermen, bears, otters and many other predators that would like to have him for dinner.

In freshwater, a physiological change takes place. His blue/black back turns olive and his shiny chrome sides take on the color of the rainbow. Traveling upstream, he uses his fat reserves, seldom feeding. He seeks out others of his kind, traveling in schools of just a few fish or hundreds at a time.

At the mouth of each tributary, he tests the water for the familiar scent that triggers his memory. Upon reaching his home stream, he may wait for weeks in the main river for the water to rise and allow him entry over the shallow gravel. Summer steelhead may enter a river in June and spawn as late as February. Winter-run fish may enter the river in December and spawn in March. Steelhead do feed in freshwater, but they are primarily living on the fat they stored up at sea.

When at last the time has come to spawn, he seeks a female and fights with other males for position over a suitable bed of gravel. The female deposits her eggs in the gravel and the male fertilize them.

When it is all over, the pair rests. Sometimes the exertion is enough to kill one or both of the mating pair. The current sweeps them downstream. Some steelhead live to make the journey to the ocean and back again. Others die after the first spawn. In death,

their decaying flesh completes the cycle of life, providing nutrients to insects, crustaceans, and fish.

To catch a steelhead, learn to read the water first. Steelhead follow the path of least resistance upstream. That might be the center of the river, but just as often it is a path along a bank or high cliff. Look for seams in the water, and foam lines, indicating the transitions of swift and slow water. Such places allow steelhead to travel with fewer obstacles.

Holding water consists of any place where a school of fish can take refuge. It might be a deep pool downstream from a riffle. It might be the pillow of water in front of a boulder. It might be the calm in the downstream shadow of a boulder. It might be a pool below a fallen tree. It will be a place where the fish can feel reasonably comfortable, and secure from predators.

Steelhead water can be 18 inches deep or 18 feet deep. It moves at walking speed with a ripple on the surface. The fish could be lying under the grass at your feet or out in the center of the river. Here the river bottom is gravel or smooth stones. Larger boulders or downed trees provide resting places on the upstream migration.

On most streams, steelhead average 24 to 30 inches in length, between four and ten pounds. Any fish that breaks the 20-pound mark is considered a trophy. Catching a steelhead of any size is a thrill for most anglers. Steelhead employ reel burning runs, high twisting leaps and dogged determination to throw the hook. Often, the fish will take to shoreside brush in an effort to escape, wrapping the line around every tree root, branch and sharp rock in its path.

Steelhead strike out of aggression, defensiveness, curiosity, hunger and sexual impulses. Successful fishermen employ, subconsciously or consciously, the techniques that trigger strikes.

Spinner Fishing

With the rain, Eagle Creek was green and running a foot higher than normal. I fished a narrow stretch on the upper river where the water swirled around a boulder and entered a deep channel between two rock ledges. It was a good spot, I had been fishing it for two hours - casting, drifting, casting again.

Downstream, an angler played a steelhead and brought it to the bank, releasing it as I watched. Raindrops pooled in the brim of my hat, forming rivulets and running into the creek.

I broke off my sand shrimp rigging and tied on the first of several spinners. The turbulent water required something heavy with a free-spinning blade that would provide more action as the lure tumbled downstream.

Standing almost at the tailout, I cast up and across, letting the lure sink. Bringing it back at about

the speed of the current, I allowed it to tumble and bump the bottom. The first fish took my homemade silver-bladed spinner, breaking the line after a brief battle. I retreated downstream.

After half an hour I worked up into the hole again, this time using a homemade brass and green spinner. My lure stopped and I raised the rod, setting the hook. The fish shook his head, then ran back and forth in the hole, coming to the surface where I could see him. He was a hook-jawed native male with a broad rainbow stripe. After five minutes he allowed me to reach down and slip the hook out of his jaw. I lifted him out for a picture, then carefully let him go to help father another generation.

One of the best fishermen I know, my uncle, friend and fishing mentor, Jon Lewis has found good success using his homemade spinners for winter and summer steelhead.

Jon likes a heavy French-bladed No. 3 for almost all rivers. He seldom puts colored tubing on the hook. "I am big on presenting a small package to

Above: Steelhead water can be 18 inches deep or 18 feet deep. It moves at walking speed with a ripple on the surface. The fish could be lying under the grass at your feet or out in the center of the river. Photo courtesy Steve's Guide Service

Left: The Skykomish River yielded a 17-pound first steelhead to this happy angler. Photo courtesy Hot Shot Guide Service

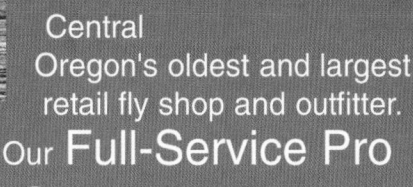

steelhead. That doesn't necessarily mean a small blade. It means a shorter body. I generally use a silver or nickel spinner in the winter with red, orange, or sometimes green tape inside the blade. I will experiment with different color accents depending on conditions." In the summer, he prefers black, green and blue accents on his spinners.

He looks for slower, deeper tailouts, or he tries to get his lure deep in the pocket water. "Don't overlook the riffles before the tailout. An example of this is at one of my favorite drifts on the Sandy River. You will see a line-up of people elbow-to-elbow fishing the deep run, and I have several times walked up to the un-fished riffle below them and had immediate success."

He stresses the importance of a slow retrieve. Reel as slow as you can. The heavier your spinner, the better you can achieve this. Experience counts. "It takes some time to get the feel for getting that spinner down, and occasionally hitting the bottom without cleaning out your vest every trip."

Part of steelhead fishing is dealing with high water. When the water is up, Jon recommends changing sizes. Use the No. 4s and 5s in high and off-colored water. "Fish closer to the bank and tight in to the boulders."

When the water is low and clear, Lewis uses No. 2s and No. 3s, depending on the current. "Low and clear in the winter usually means cold water, so you still need to get down and in their face," Jon said. "I'm not scared of using bright spinners (silver) in clear water - just keep it small and put it on their nose."

He searches out classic steelhead water. "I look for a spot with a current that is close to walking speed with a little chop on the surface. If there is a boulder or two, so much the better. I start at the head of the hole and work my way to the tailout."

Low water calls for a change in tactics. Approach the fish from behind so that the fish is quartering away. Cast upstream and let the lure tumble a little with the retrieve. Keep it just barely spinning and work the spinner to force the fish into taking it or backing off.

Confidence is one of the most important tools that an angler can bring to steelhead water

There is no magic to enticing a steelhead to take a spinner. Rather, a steelhead will hit a spinner for one reason. Big fish like their space. Let a flashy interloper into their living room and they will react in one of three ways. One, pretend it doesn't exist. Two, run away from it. Or, three, destroy it. The only way a big fish can kill a smaller creature is to crush it in his mouth. This is the response the fisherman wants to provoke.

The fisherman's job is to elicit a strike before the fish are spooked and run away. I believe that any fish that can be spotted can be caught. That's why I always use polarized glasses to cut the glare on the water. If I can see the fish before they see me then I can plan a stalk.

There should be a variety of spinners in your box. Start with the minimum flash that you believe is necessary to move a fish into striking. In low water that might be a tarnished brass or black-bladed lure. In deeper water that might mean a shiny brass blade or even a silver-plated lure in a muddy river. It is a fine

line between enough shine to make them chase it and so much that it spooks them.

I believe you can aggravate fish into striking. That is why you can cast to holding fish for an hour, then switch to something flashy and one will streak from across the run to slam it.

Maximize the time that the spinner is in front of the fish. That means a tantalizingly slow retrieve. Just fast enough that the blade spins. Rarely will a fish take a spinner that doesn't spin. In the case of fish holding in a riffle - cast from downstream and bring the spinner straight toward them, just above the speed of the water. They will have no choice but to hit it or get out of the way.

Treat it as a logical process, understand the reasons why a fish will hit one spinner when nothing else will work. There's nothing mystical about enticing a steelhead to bite, but there is magic in what happens after you set the hook.

When fishing different rivers around the Northwest, an ability to read water is an important

Above: There is no substitute for the ability to understand where steelhead will hold in any given stretch of river. Photo courtesy Jon Lewis

skill. River bottoms are in a constant state of change as boulders shift, trees fall, fallen trees decay, and floods expose gravel bars or fill pools with silt. Holes that produced good fishing the year before can be completely changed after a high-water year. There is no substitute for the ability to understand where steelhead will hold in any given stretch of river.

No summer is complete without a couple of steelheading trips to the lower Deschutes River. One August day I went fishing with my good friend Troy Neimann. We arrived later than usual. By the time we hit the river, it was 12:30 in the afternoon.

We headed up the trail, smelling the blackberries, the sage, and the dust on the wind that funneled down the canyon.

We started on a run where the river flows from two to eight feet deep. It's textbook spinner water with submerged boulders providing shelter for up-running fish.

There may be steelhead anywhere in the river, but the most hook-ups go to the angler who studies the water. Look for the channels that the fish will use to move upstream. The path of least resistance. It takes effort to move through the fast water. Often, you can find fish resting in the tailout of the hole above a long set of rapids. Spend the most time fishing the holding water just above the main channel.

If there are boulders, so much the better. The upstream bulge and the downstream shadow can provide protection from the current for one or more steelhead. These resting places are prime targets for the spinner fisherman.

It was an hour and a half later when I switched to a nickel-plated spinner with red beads. The inside of the blade was decorated with flat black tape. I had seen the combination work before on a bright summer day. I moved up into a riffle where the river was channelized by rocky runs.

Working close to shore, I was rewarded with a strike that almost ripped the rod from my hands. The fish streaked across the river and made a series of jumps before turning and running toward me. Reeling crazily, I managed to keep the slack out of the line. It ran downstream, then out again before it let me guide it to the shore. An eight-pound native, I slipped the hook out. Troy took a picture and we let it go.

It was almost four in the afternoon when the second one took my blue and silver spinner. She dragged my six-pound Maxima through a rocky ledge and streaked across the river while my line sawed lava. Slowly I gathered the line back, then eased up on the pressure, hoping she would move upstream and free herself from the rock. It didn't work. After ten minutes, I tightened the drag and put more pressure on my rod than I thought it would take.

The fish came off the ledge like a shot and I could see her for the first time now, just 30 feet off my rod tip, thrashing and wallowing, running downstream. Easing off on the drag to compensate for the frayed line, I guided her into the shallows and saw that this was a hatchery fish. One for the table.

As I carried my steelhead back to the truck, we couldn't help but wonder how many we would have hooked if we had been there earlier in the day.

Above: There may be steelhead anywhere in the river, but the most hook-ups go to the angler who studies the water.
Photo by Gary Lewis

Spoon Fishing

A spoon is a wobbling lure usually made from hammered brass and finished in a variety of colors. They are easy to use, but more difficult to master.

Spoons are best fished on spinning gear. An eight or nine foot rod is appropriate. Use eight-pound line in the summer and ten or 12-pound line in the winter on a reel big enough to hold 200 yards of line. Attach a high-quality snap swivel to the spoon and tie the lure directly to your main line. A leader isn't necessary.

Present the spoon slower than current speed on the level where fish are holding. The spoon should wobble, not spin, to afford the most flash. Hold your rod tip high, or lower it, reel in or give line to keep the lure wobbling, not spinning, about 18 inches above the bottom.

Being successful with spoons requires learning the feel of the lure in different types of water. It is an effective technique that is versatile and can be used under various conditions.

Float Fishing

Float fishing employs a spinning rod and reel with a feathered jig and a balsa wood float. That's all you need.

Start with a 1/8-ounce jig tied to the main line with a balsa float positioned above it. Adjust the float so the jig runs at or above the level of the fish. Best bet is to set the jig to run 18- to 24-inches off the bottom. The float keeps the jig suspended so the angler loses less gear. When the fish takes the lure, the drifting float stops, sinks, or runs upstream. All the fisherman has to do is set the hook and hold on.

Color and size make a difference to the fish. Keep an assortment of 1/8- and 1/4-ounce jigs in red, hot pink, and pink/white for winter steelhead. For summer fish, carry blue, as well as black and black/chartreuse. Where legal, tipping the jig with sand shrimp or eggs will help to tip the odds in your favor.

Besides being a technique that is easy to master, jig fishing is easier on the fish than many other methods. The fish elevates to take the lure, and is usually hooked in the roof or the corner of the mouth, allowing for a quick release if the fish must be returned to the river.

Plugging

Fishing with diving plugs for steelhead is an art that, when developed, will help you put more fish in the boat.

It may seem easy to the fellow holding the rod, but the fellow holding the rod isn't doing the fishing, he's just holding the rod. The real talent is the man or woman who is running the boat.

The person on the oars must learn his boat well, and come to know the river. Length of line out, style of diving plug, current vagaries and presentation speed are just a few of the variables the boat operator must take into account.

Strikes are cued by feeding impulses, or defense as the plug backs the big fish downstream.

Bank anglers can also catch fish with diving plugs. Hot Shots, Flatfish and Kwikfish are some of the Northwest favorites. Cast at a downstream angle and let the tension of the line force the diver down. Reel to make it dive deeper or feed line to allow it to rise. Speed of retrieve is important. And slower is better.

Drift Fishing

Drift fishing with cured salmon or steelhead eggs or other baits is still one of the most popular methods on Oregon and Washington rivers. It is a technique that the well-rounded steelheader should learn, but it is not for the beginner. Drift fishing requires a sensitive touch that is best learned by experience, after you have caught a number of steelhead using other techniques.

The best water for using drift gear has a gravel or stony bottom with a current that moves at about the speed of a fast walk. The bottom should have few impediments to the drift.

Tie leaders to present the bait at the level where fish hold. It might be 18 inches, it might be 36 inches, depending upon such factors as the speed of the current, water clarity, and depth. Start with a No. 4 - No. 1/0 bait hook and tie an egg loop knot to secure the bait.

Slide a cork bobber on the leader then tie the leader to a barrel swivel. There are many ways to attach the weight to the line, but one of the more popular techniques employs surgical tubing. Cut a one-inch length of tubing and slide the tubing over the main line. Next, insert a section of pencil lead weight into the tubing. The lead can be trimmed when less weight is needed, or replaced with a longer lead when you need more weight.

Since the weight is the most often snagged item in your gear, the tubing allows you to pull up and lose only the weight to a snag.

Cast upstream and pick up the slack. Hold the rod tip at 11 o'clock. The weight should bounce along the bottom, transmitting a tap-tap-tap to the rod tip. When the bite comes, it is often a soft

Above: Dylan Casaday with a fly-caught Deschutes River Steelhead. Photo courtesy The Fly Box Outfitters

mouthing of the bait that stops the ticking of the weight, or a quick pull on your line. Set the hook by lifting the rod tip back over your head.

Side-drifting bait entails a similar rigging, but the fishing is done from a boat. Anglers should place their baits in the seam where steelhead are expected to hold. The person running the boat should keep the boat moving at the speed of the drifting baits. This method holds the bait in the productive water for a longer period of time.

Fly Fishing

I caught my first steelhead when Ronald Reagan was in his first term and I have caught a bunch of them since. But precious few of those were landed on fly tackle. I've fly fished for trout for 20 years but have seldom employed fur and feathers for steelhead.

So when pro guide Al Bagley offered to show me the fishing on the Warm Springs side of the Deschutes River, I jumped at the chance to learn the finer points of steelhead 'swing' technique from an expert.

Bagley started his business with the blessing of the Warm Springs Tribal Council in 1997. His is the only fishing guide service to operate on Indian land. His enthusiasm for catching trout and steelhead on the fly, plus the opportunity to see the river from a different point-of-view, has made Bagley's business successful. So much so, that Governor Kitzhaber awarded him the 2002

Minority Enterprise Development Award for a Service Business.

Fresh snow crowned the hills and the sky promised more to come. Today, we would fish with Cobby Shadley, Bagley's nephew, who had recently begun to work for River Bend Guide Service. Since there were two guides and only one guided, both Cobby and Al would get a lot of fishing in.

Al watched from the bank as I cast, mended, swung and stepped (stumbled) downstream, trying to get into the rhythm of the river. Downstream, Cobby landed and released a steelhead. Al helped me refine my technique. Soon, he was headed upstream. "You fish here," he told me, pointing to the best run. "I'll go up around the corner. By the time I get to that tree there," he said, pointing, "I'll have a fish on." And it was so. Al landed and released a native steelhead, and we moved on.

At the next hole, I cast, mended, swung, stepped, stumbled and snagged in the brush behind me. Al coached, unhooked flies from trees, grass, and bushes. A kingfisher watched from a nearby perch, unimpressed.

We moved downstream again, and Al pointed to a riffle and told me how to fish it. It was coming together now: cast, mend, swing, step, cast, mend, swing, step. Fish on. I saw it flash and roll, breaking the water with its dorsal fin. Then my line went limp.

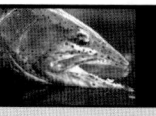

Gear Up For Spinning

Use an eight to ten-foot medium-action spinning rod. Water conditions can range from low and clear, to high and muddy. A spinning reel equipped with adjustable drag, and 200 yards of six to ten-pound test is best for this type of fishing.

Carry a wide selection of spinners to fit the conditions. French-bladed spinners sized No. 3 and No. 4, will see the most action, but No. 2s and No. 5s should be carried and used depending on water clarity and turbulence. Silver, brass, nickel, and black plated blades and bodies are the most common finishes. In winter, try spinners accented with reds, oranges, pinks, and greens.

Tie the spinner to a 24-inch leader and barrel swivel, or directly to your main line with an improved clinch knot. Fish it low and slow.

Whether you choose hardware or feathered creations to tempt steelhead, treat it as a logical process and understand the reasons why fish strike. There's nothing mystical about enticing steelhead to bite, but there is magic in what happens after you set the hook.

Left: Eli Rico with a big Klickitat River steelhead. Photo courtesy Hot Shot Guide Service

Cast, mend, swing. Fish on. By the time, I had completed the run I had landed two steelhead and hooked one more.

Any steelhead is a good steelhead, but Al had told me I was going to hook a runner (he's always making predictions) and I hoped he was right. I kept fishing. Downstream, I landed a third steelhead, admired it and let it go.

The next fish hit like a sledgehammer and ran like a freight train through my fly line and into the backing, making the reel sing. Burning downstream through the riffle, he ran, through another hole and into the next riffle. I began to wonder if I would ever see that fly line again.

I ran, stumbled, fell in up to my chest, got up, fell again, clutching at branches with my left hand,
trying to keep the tip up with my right hand. I gained a little line back as the river swept me along. And I watched the sole from my right boot float away, torn off by a sharp rock.

Almost three hundred yards downstream, I caught up to my fly line and the fish. It shook its head and took off on another run, snapping my leader. I never saw that steelhead, but I will never forget it.

Fly fishing is best in the evening and in the morning until the sun has been on the water for two hours. Midday fishing requires different tactics. The fish are less likely to move as far for a fly when the sun is on the water, so a sink-tip line is in order, to put the fly closer to the fish.

Two main fly fishing techniques are used for steelhead. The swing technique presents the fly to every fish within casting range and elicits strikes from the most aggressive and curious steelhead.

Be careful to not wade too far, too fast. Steelhead can hold in very shallow water, close to the bank. Work the water close to the bank first. Wade in at the top of the run and make the first cast at a downstream angle.

Make one upstream mend then hold the rod tip at a 45-degree angle while the current sweeps the line and fly downstream. Let the fly swing directly downstream. Let it hang, then strip it in. Take two steps downstream, then cast again.

Spey rods are becoming increasingly popular among steelheaders. They slow down the fly's drift, and give the fisherman more control. On a big, brawling river, the two-handed rod also lets you cast farther and cover more water.

Whether you use a spey rod or not, maximize the time that your offering is in front of the fish. The trick is to get the fly close to the bottom, in front of fish, and that means using fast-sinking lines like the Teeny or Orvis Depth Charge lines.

Top Right: A wild Deschutes River steelhead. Photo courtesy Jon Lindsay

Right: The Hoh River gave up this nice steelhead to Adam Harberg. Photo courtesy Scott Cook, Fly and Field Guide Service

Left: Maximize the time your lure is in front of the fish and slow down your retrieve. Photo by Gary Lewis

Good patterns for fishing on the swing are Articulated Leeches, Wooly Buggers, and other streamer patterns.

Something will entice a strike. The worst that can happen is that you will spook them and sometimes even spooked fish will strike out of aggression or defense.

The other popular steelhead fly technique is called nymphing. Steelheaders fish No. 8 and larger weighted nymphs beneath strike indicators. This is a great technique for use in pocket water and in the upper stretches of some Northwest rivers.

When salmon are spawning, you can sometimes catch steelhead, downstream in the riffles, by drifting roe imitations like the Egg Fly, Van Luven and Umpqua Special.

Whether you use flies, bait, spoons, spinners, plugs, or a jig and bobber, you can bring more fish to the bank. It comes down to observation, taking notes, reading water and learning how steelhead react to different stimuli in different situations.

Confidence is one of the most important tools that an angler can bring to steelhead water. It is one of those commodities that come only with time spent on the river, and success.

If you like catching wild steelhead, you'll also like letting them go to spawn, ensuring that there will always be steelhead in our winter rivers. Since wild steelhead must be released in many Oregon and Washington streams, you should use gear that

won't hook them deep. You should bring the fish in quickly and release them carefully.

Listing the steelhead rivers in Oregon and Washington would fill several pages. Some of Oregon's better known streams are the Wilson, Elk, Sixes, Siletz, Clackamas, Nehalem, Nestucca, Chetco, Umpqua, Grande Ronde, Deschutes, Sandy, and the Rogue. Plenty of other Oregon rivers have great runs of steelhead as well.

In Washington, the lower Columbia, Bogachiel, Calawah, Skagit, Stillaguamish, Cowlitz, Kalama, North Fork Lewis, East Fork Lewis, Grande Ronde, Quillayute, Queets, Quinault, Hoh, Humptulips, Skykomish, Klickitat, Wind, Washougal and a host of other rivers provide good fishing.

SALMON

Five species of salmon are indigenous to our corner of North America. Chinook, silver, pink, chum, and sockeye all make their home in Oregon and Washington. Freshwater salmon fishing can be found in either state in almost any month of the year.

Salmon roam through the northern Pacific, following the feed. Hatchery-reared or wild-born, the salmon makes an epic journey. Some salmon log up to 3,500 miles on their round-trip journey. From ocean to native stream, it may travel hundreds of miles on energy stored over three or four years at sea.

In general, salmon spawn in late summer and fall, then hatch in the spring. Species differ in timing of the runs, but may share the same river for weeks leading up to the spawn.

As food, there are few fish prized as highly as salmon. Our Northwest fish are processed and sent far and wide across the earth to feed those not fortunate enough to live here. For sportsmen, they are a particularly interesting quarry as timing of the run, proper gear and bait selection, water reading skill, presentation, and strength all are required to subdue a salmon.

Photo by Brian O'Keefe

Chinook (King) Salmon

Lightning flashed and thunder rolled across the tops of the hills. Rain pounded down, soaking my cotton shirt to my skin. We were working our spinners through a section of pocket water two miles up from the river's mouth. Alan, who had landed two fish the day before, was on my left and Ryan Eicher, who had caught one that morning, was on my right.

The top of a boulder jutted out of the water twenty feet in front of me, creating shelter from the current. I cast a No. 5 Blue Fox spinner behind the rock, letting the current take it, reeling as it swept downstream. The tip of my rod transmitted the slow beat of the blade and suddenly it stopped and I felt the unmistakable shake of a head and set the hook. Line peeled off the reel as the fish broke out into the current, heading back to the Columbia. Just as suddenly, it was over and the fish was gone.

Reeling the spinner in, I smiled, remembering the last chinook I had hooked in this stretch of the river while fishing for steelhead. That one took my spinner and 175 yards of 12-pound test line before breaking off at the spool.

42 miles up from the mouth is the river's focal point for salmon fishermen. Sherars Falls gathers the might and power of the river into a narrow channel carved through a lava flow. The chinook stack up in the whitewater just below the falls. Here, Indians fish from shaky platforms with dip nets, just as they have for years. If you go, just watching them fish is worth the trip.

Anglers have success using fresh roe, prawns, and tuna balls. The water here is deep and turbulent, so heavy tackle is required to reach the fish.

I found myself alone on the river, fishing my way back to camp as the sun set on the western rim. A freight train, on the far wall, wound out of the gorge, its horn a mournful wail in the windy, desert canyon. I sat in the grass, watching, listening to the clack and whine of the wheels on the twin iron ribbons and thought about why I had come here.

Sometimes these salmon are like that train. Suddenly they are there, and for a few moments you are connected, the line peeling away, your drag whining in protest. And some fish, unstoppable, will just keep going, taking and breaking your tackle in the process.

Chinook will average 15 pounds, but 20- and 30-pound fish are common. And every year a few lucky fishermen boat 40- and 50-pound fish. But chinook salmon do grow bigger. The largest ever caught (by a commercial fisherman) weighed 126 pounds.

Fresh from the salt, this salmon has a blue-green back that darkens to black on top and silvery sides. Scattered across its back and sides above the lateral line, it has large, uneven black spots. Its tail is completely spotted and its teeth are set in black gums. As the chinook approaches the spawning season, females turn brassy in color, then black. Males develop hooked jaws and turn red and green, then black.

Oregon and Washington's spring-run chinook, also called springers, enter the freshwater as early as January. They make their way upriver where they will eventually spawn in late summer and early fall. During this time, they live on the energy reserves they built up while at sea, rarely eating. The fishing peaks in May and June.

Once they hit freshwater, the salmon undergo changes brought on by the change in their environment. For the first couple of weeks they retain their silvery sides, but the freshwater seems to tarnish the fish and the silver turns brass or black the longer

Right: This big, upriver bright fall chinook was spawned by Mount Hood Community College students at the Little White Salmon National Fish Hatchery in Washington. Photo courtesy Mount Hood Community College

the fish is in freshwater. Their existence, which used to revolve around food, now centers around procreation. Social, they run in schools of a few fish to hundreds, like so many High School students at a pizza joint after the big game. They may hold in one hole for several days or a week. Then when fresh rain raises the river level, off they go again.

Many holes hold fish year after year, but sometimes it seems as if the fish pass by places where you found them last year. There is a lot we don't know about salmon, but it could be they are more social than we give them credit for. Maybe the first fish up the river didn't stop in one hole and didn't leave their scent. Chances are, the next fish won't stop there either. Keep track of where you find fish early in the season.

As the time to spawn draws near, the hens leave the deep water in search of swift, gravel-bottomed riffles. Bucks follow, sensing the time is near. Often, several males will battle each other for the privilege of mating. The female searches for, then selects a site and turns on her side to dig a nest or redd in which to sow her eggs. With her tail she sweeps the gravel clean while she digs a trough about 12 inches deep. As she deposits her eggs, the dominant male comes alongside and releases his milt. Salmon produce between 2500 and 7000 eggs. After spawning, the salmon die and their flesh becomes food for the other creatures of the river.

The fry, after absorbing their egg sacs begin to forage for food while trying to keep from becoming food for birds and other fish. They change color as they grow. As fingerlings, they are speckled and marked with fingernail-sized "parr" marks. As smolts, in the five- to seven-inch range, they lose their parr marks and become small, silvery versions of their parents, heading out to sea.

Chinook stay in the ocean for two to seven years, feeding on crustaceans, squid, mollusks, and baitfish. The slowest to mature are the ones that grow biggest and truly deserve the appellation of "king salmon."

Tactics

Most fishermen catch their first fish under a bobber. But, for many, once the fundamentals are mastered, bobber fishing is left behind. As I sat in my uncle's drift boat, watching my bobber, I wondered what would happen if a salmon actually took the bait.

It was September and the fall chinook were in the Kalama. We were anchored, using cured eggs from August's steelhead, suspended ten feet beneath a cork float.

Here the river deepens at a sweeping 90-degree bend, washing around a gravel bar on the inside of the turn and a rock ledge on the outside. Our baits drifted out of the light-green water and into the dark-green depths. We free-spooled our reels, backing line out to ensure natural drift. This was where the fish would be.

When I was a kid, my thoughts often wandered, as would my gaze, leaving the bobber for a moment to look at the trees or watch a bird. I'm older now, but still prone to distraction. I'm not sure what caught my attention, but when I looked back, my float had disappeared. Looking into the green water, I saw it, six feet under.

Left: There are few fish prized as highly as our spring salmon. Timing of run, proper gear and bait selection, presentation, skill and strength are required to subdue a spring chinook. Photo courtesy Troy Neimann

I raised the rod in an arc over my head, setting the hook. The battle was on. In the boat, we were able to follow the fish as it ran back and forth in the hole. Soon we were able to slip the net beneath a fine fall chinook.

Chinook are the first fall salmon to arrive, showing up in late August, and moving back and forth across the bar. September is the prime time to intercept these runs and good fishing can continue into the first week of November.

When the fish are in the bays, staging for their upriver run, many anglers use a mooching rig with cut herring or small whole herring. Start with 30-pound main line and tie on a 3-way swivel. Tie 20 inches of leader to one eye and attach a snap swivel. This leg will hold the weight. Tie two to four feet of 25-pound leader to the other leg, then attach a bead chain swivel. To the bead chain, tie another four feet of leader, terminating at two 2/0 hooks. Herring is hooked through nose and tail and should spin in the water. Run it deep with heavy lead, keeping your herring close to the fish. Position your bait so that it rides at or slightly above the level of the fish. Fish deeper than the fish and you won't catch a thing.

Change tactics when the fish move into tidewater. The best fishing may be had an hour before, to an hour after the tide changes. Troll large rainbow pattern or chartreuse spinners in No. 6 and No. 7. Red and nickel is another good spinner combination. Fish it slow, two to four feet from the bottom. Or rig a Kwikfish with a herring filet. Use 1-1/2 ounces of lead to keep your spinner or Kwikfish two feet off the bottom.

Other anglers use spoons in tidewater. The Luhr Jensen Company recommends running spoons with red or metallic finishes closer to the surface, yellow and chartreuse at medium depths. In deeper water, only blues and greens are distinguishable to the fish. Blues and greens can be effective at any depth though, since those are the colors of many baitfish.

Another technique that pays off for some anglers is fly-fishing for salmon stacked in tidewater, waiting for rain. Baitfish imitations like the Franke Shiner or Deceiver patterns can be very effective. The trick is to use a fast-sinking fly line and flashy bait-fish imitations. Cast beyond the fish then let the fly sink. Retrieve with long, slow strips.

September rains bring the salmon out of tidewater and up into the river. Target these up-running fish as the water begins to drop. It's time to change tactics again. Look for deep runs and shaded pools where these big fish can rest and recover before they head upstream again. Spoons and spinners will be even more effective now, as fish become more aggressive and territorial.

In most rivers, the key is rainfall. Get ready to go when it starts to rain and waters rise. Fish will be moving upstream when the water colors. When the water turns from brown, back to green, that is the best time to be on the water.

The same spinners you used in tidewater can be put to use upstream. Instead of trolling, or casting and retrieving, these spinners are fished in place. Find the slots where upriver kings travel, then ambush them with a well-positioned spinner.

Photo by Brian O'Keefe

Employ a two- to eight- ounce sinker on a dropper to hold the lure in place.

Driftboaters favor back-bouncing bait and back-trolling salmon plugs such as the Hot Shot. These techniques work the best on holding fish. Back the boat downstream while bouncing a lead and bait rig through fish-holding water. Lift the rod, then give line as needed to keep the lead bouncing and the bait drifting back to waiting fish. Set the hook when the line goes limp or breaks from the flow of the current.

Many different baits work well for back-bouncers. Salmon roe is most popular, but sand shrimp, herring, and prawns also work well. Some anglers are having success using fluorescent rubber worms and grubs.

When fishing a Hot Shot or similar lure, tie the line directly to the eye snap for best action. Also, use lighter line if you want the lure to dive deeper. Heavy line creates more drag, preventing the lure from diving as deep. The technique is effective because, like in back-bouncing, the drift boater backs fish down with the lure, daring them to strike or get out of the way.

Fish spoons and spinners slow in deeper holes and in the tail-outs of pools when fish are moving. As the water clears, switch to drifting small baits, fishing bobber and bait, or feathered jigs.

Fall is made for fishing. Water temperatures are just right for steelhead activity and autumn rains have raised rivers, allowing fish to pass.

Fish can still be caught on any stream when the water is high and muddy. To protect energy reserves and avoid heavy, gill-damaging silt, fish will move to the bank to find calm water. Often, you can find these fish by casting nearly into the shore-side brush or spotting fins and tails of fish hiding in six inches of water.

When the water is muddy, drifting salmon eggs or sand shrimp is effective for taking kings. Fishing bait under bobbers is very productive in tidewater, and upstream, when water is lower and fish stack up in deep holes.

Oregon has great chinook salmon fishing in many rivers. Some of the top prospects include the Columbia, Clackamas, Deschutes, Umpqua, North Umpqua, Willamette River, Rogue River, Sandy, Wilson, Salmon, Trask, and Nestucca.

Chinook salmon can also be found in many Washington waters. Some of the top prospects include the Columbia, Cowlitz, North Fork Lewis River, Washougal, Hoh, Drano Lake, Naselle, and the Quillayute system.

Before you fish, read the Sport Fishing Regulations for restrictions specific to the water you're fishing.

Knot a 3-way swivel to your 12- to 30-pound main line and attach 24-36 inches of leader terminating at a 1/0-4/0 single hook. Attach a sinker (1/4 to 4 ounces) to the other leg of the swivel. Fix an adjustable bobber to the mainline. Fish the bait at or slightly above where fish are holding in the water column, typically two to four feet off the bottom. Pay close attention to your float. Bites can be powerful, but may also be soft. At the slightest movement, set the hook.

Reel-burning runs, aerial acrobatics, surface rolls, and deep-water dogging tactics are all part of the chinook's bag of tricks. Battles can last an hour or more if the fish is big.

It is rare to hook a freshwater fish that has the absolute power to make a mockery of the tackle designed to subdue it. But the opportunity exists whenever you match your brains against the brawn of the chinook salmon.

Coho (Silver) Salmon

There is urgency in autumn, a need to go and do. Days are shortening, and in the far north, geese and ducks are forming into flocks and beginning their migration south. My wife reminds me that there is firewood to chop, and I suddenly remember that there is no better time than fall for fishing.

Images spring to mind and I remember standing in the Kalama in a downpour, silver salmon pushing through the shallows at the head of the rapids, the tops of their backs cutting wakes in the smooth water.

Fall is made for fishing. Water temperatures are just right for steelhead activity and autumn rains have raised rivers, allowing fish to pass. In many rivers, steelhead, cohos, and kings share the water in the months of October. And many of the people who

shared summer angling are gone now that school is back in session and hunting seasons have begun.

In October, coho salmon are the main event in many Oregon and Washington rivers. Cohos, also known as silvers, have silver sides and a dark back, stippled with small dark spots. Only the top lobe of the tail has spots. The teeth are set in whitish gums. After they re-enter freshwater on their spawning run, the males turn green and red while the females' chrome turns to black.

Every year, a few silvers are caught that tip the scales above 20 pounds, but most average in the five to ten-pound class. They rival chinook salmon in popularity due to their numbers and their willingness to take bait and lure.

There are two runs of silvers in many Northwest rivers. The first fish enter freshwater in late August and early September. The latter run peaks in October and November, but good fishing can continue into the first part of December.

Tactics for catching silvers change depending on the stage of the run. While fish are fresh from the salt, herring rigs can be used successfully. Float fishing with cured salmon eggs is also effective in tidewater. Many anglers are successful trolling Hot Shots, Wiggle Warts, and similar diving plugs up and downstream in the lower reaches of the river. Others free-drift eggs. Spoons and green or blue spinners are also productive.

As the fish move upriver, closer to spawning beds, they are more easily taken with spoons and spinners. Lures like the 1/4-ounce white Rooster

Tail, the nickel and green, or nickel and red Blue Fox are consistent producers on these fish. When using spinners and spoons, the slower your retrieve the better. Jigs produce for silver salmon as well, with purple and pink, and red and white being the favorites. Fish with weighted marabou jigs under a float. Set the distance between float and jig such that the jig will be at the level of the fish, usually six to 24 inches off the bottom. Watch the downstream drift of the bobber, then set the hook if the float is taken down or starts streaking upstream.

When pursuing silvers in the upper rivers, gear fishermen are well-served by an 8-to 9-foot graphite rod. Use a high-quality spinning reel that holds at least 200 yards of 8-to 12-pound test line.

Fly fishermen should use a 7- to 9-weight, 9-foot fly rod with a high-density sink tip line. Weighted streamer patterns in red, orange, pink, purple, white and chartreuse work well for silvers. Carry a selection of shrimp and egg flies, as well.

Jack salmon (chinook under 24 inches, and silvers under 20 inches) provide another opportunity for salmon fishermen. They can be targeted by casting No. 3 and No. 4 french bladed, green spinners or fishing a whole nightcrawler with a bit of fluorescent green yarn on a No. 4 worm hook.

Look for silvers in shallow flats with moderate current. Unlike chinook, you can often find large numbers of silvers along current seams, the mouths of small tributaries, in the smooth-water tongue above rapids, and near boulders and submerged timber.

There are few better ways to spend your time than in pursuit of silver salmon. As your breath turns to vapor in the crisp morning air, remember this:

fishing always beats chopping firewood.

The list of Washington's best rivers for silver salmon is long. In southwest Washington, fish the Cowlitz, the Kalama, and North Fork Lewis. The Puyallup

Left: Greg McDonald cradles a Lake Washington sockeye salmon. Photo courtesy Hot Shot Guide Service

River, Snohomish system, and the Willapa Bay Tributaries are other good bets.

In Oregon, the Clackamas, Nehalem, Rogue River, Umpqua and North Umpqua, among other rivers, are consistent producers of good runs of silver salmon.

Pink Salmon

Pink salmon enter Washington rivers in August and September, with the run hitting its peak in early October. In Washington, the runs generally occur only in odd-numbered years. Pinks (also called humpbacks or humpies) head for the ocean soon after hatching and absorbing the yolk sac. This smallest of the Pacific salmon species returns to their native rivers as two year-olds. Depending on ocean conditions and other factors, pinks average between two and eight pounds as adults.

Pinks have smaller scales than other salmon. Large, black, oval spots on the back and tail are another distinguishing characteristic. Also, males develop a pronounced hump on their backs prior to spawning.

In the river, they favor deep pools. Many fish will congregate in one hole and can be seen jumping and cavorting as they ready for the mating ritual. When the time is right, spawning occurs in the gravelly shallows, often not far above tidewater.

Wobbling spoons, spinners, drift gear, bait and flies are all good bets for pinks. A high-density sink tip line is important for the fly fisherman.

Washington's best pink salmon runs occur, in odd-numbered years, in the lower Skagit River, and in the Snohomish system. Other Puget Sound

Above: Scott Cook with a big chum salmon from the Kilchis River. Photo courtesy Scott Cook, Fly and Field Guide Service

rivers also receive runs of pink salmon. Read the current regulations before angling for pink salmon.

Sockeye

The sockeye salmon, fresh from the salt, is a silver-sided fish with a grayish blue back and small black spots. After a short time in freshwater, the female turns red or olive. The male's head turns green, its jaw begins to hook, its body turns a bright red, and its back humps almost like a pink salmon.

Sea-run sockeye (also called red salmon) average between four and seven pounds. They hit the river between June and September, spawning in October and November. Hard fighters when hooked, sockeyes are well-known for being hard to catch in

Left: Phil Simpson with a 24 pound Skykomish River chum salmon. Photo courtesy Hot Shot Guide Service.

freshwater. However, anglers can catch sockeyes with spoons, spinners, jigs, and flies.

Sockeye salmon are seldom found south of the Columbia River system. Lake Washington sometimes hosts sockeye runs. The Baker, Skagit, and Sol Duc rivers are good bets for sockeye salmon. Check regulations prior to fishing for sockeyes. For information on kokanee (landlocked sockeye salmon), see the Kokanee chapter.

Chum Salmon

Most runs of chum salmon enter the freshwater late in the season, after many other runs of salmon have ended. Some fish spawn in the lower reaches of their home river, but many will travel far upstream to spawn. Fresh from the salt, chums (also called dog salmon) look like small chinooks. They begin to change color when they have been in fresh a few days.

A faint reddish, purple, blue, and olive green mottling appears on its sides and becomes more vivid the longer the fish is in freshwater. Its back turns black and, in males, the hook on the lower jaw becomes more pronounced. Like all of the Pacific salmon, chums die after spawning, their decaying flesh enriching the water of their native streams.

While still quite small, soon after their yolk sacs are absorbed, the parr make their way to the ocean where they spend almost the entirety of their lives. They return to freshwater as three, four or five year-olds. Chums average between five and fifteen pounds in Washington and Oregon rivers, though a few of the big tackle-busters have been known to tip the scales at more than 20 pounds.

When you time the run right, chums are not all that hard to catch. Remember, go small and chartreuse. The larger baits that work well for chinooks and silvers do not do as well for chums. When using drift gear, start with a chartreuse Corky and a little tuft of chartreuse yarn knotted to your egg loop knot. When chartreuse isn't working, try red, orange, pink, or white. Use stout gear because these fish can pull. Many anglers prefer to use 12-15 pound test line and a rod with plenty of backbone.

Spinners and spoons are also effective for chums. Alaskan anglers like the Pixie - a nickel-plated spoon with red or green accents.

Fly rodders should use an 8 or 9-weight rod loaded with a high-density sink-tip line for presenting the fly in deeper water. Carry a spare spool, rigged with a floating line in case fish are encountered in shallower water. Go prepared with plenty of backing. Small streamer patterns and shrimp imitations work well for chums. Best colors, again, are chartreuse, red, orange, pink, and white.

In Oregon, chums are found in the Miami and Kilchis Rivers.

The best Washington streams are the Skykomish, Dosewallips, Duckabush, Nisqually, Skokomish, and the West Fork Satsop rivers. Check your regulations before fishing.

STURGEON

Bruised and sullen storm clouds swept overhead. Standing in the river sand on Woodland Bar, we set our faces in the squall, pulled hats tight and watched the tips of the sturgeon rods.

We were using pickled roll mop herring and sand shrimp. My brother-in-law, Shannon Winters, asked if I wanted the pickle as he pulled a herring fillet and a dill wedge from the jar. I wrinkled my nose. He tied the bait on a 5/0 hook and 14-inch leader. A six-ounce pyramid weight would keep the bait on the bottom. Shannon took a bite from the pickle (not recommended) for luck.

We set the baits and put the rods in their holders, tightening the line so that a strike would telegraph to the rod tip.

The first bite was a gentle tap-tap-tap. I slipped the rod from the holder. Ready to set the hook when I felt the fish. Nothing. After some time, I set the rod in the pipe again and backed up. There. Another bite. I eased the rod out and waited for the pull of the fish moving away with the herring. Nothing. Reeling in, we found the fish had sucked

Above: A big sturgeon at the boat. It's important to bring the big ones to the boat as soon as possible so less stress is put on the mighty fish. Photo courtesy Outdoors NW

the bait off the hook. Shannon re-baited and took another bite of the pickle.

The river is narrow between Woodland and Columbia City. Taking turns watching the rods, we scanned the far shore and watched gulls flying against the stormy sky.

Then, out of the clouds, an eagle wheeled, diving hard at an osprey. The smaller bird rolled away from the attack, losing altitude. On the wind, another osprey appeared, wings folded, driving down against the back of the eagle.

Thus outnumbered, the eagle fought a valiant retreat while under continuous assault from above and below. We forgot our fishing rods, watching the battle until the birds were mere specks upriver.

Something was pecking at our baits and getting away with a free dinner. Peamouth, suckers, sculpin, or squawfish might have been the culprits.

The sun slipped beyond the hills and darkness rushed in. Shannon closed his tackle boxes against the rain and carried them to the truck.

Tap-tap. I took the rod from its holder, waiting for the fish to come back or the word from Shannon to reel in and put the rods away. I waited. Shannon watched.

Something pulled. I set the hook, sweeping the ten-foot rod through a long, backward arc, and backing up the beach. The rod bent with the heaviness that meant there was a sturgeon at the other end and not some lesser fish. The line cut upstream, then the fish broke water, head and tail showing sixty yards out.

I set the rod butt against my thigh and gained line. Soon the fish was swimming parallel to the beach. Holding the rod high, I stepped in and brought it to the water's edge.

Unhooking the sturgeon, I cradled it for the camera then slowly rocked it back and forth in the water. With a mighty kick, the fish was away, its studded back and forked tail disappearing into the dark river.

Even as I was returning my last sturgeon to the water, I was looking forward to my next chance to hook one of these dinosaurs of the deep.

For several years, my Uncle had been telling me of the big sturgeon that he was boating in the middle Columbia. A month after my Woodland Bar sturgeon, I found myself in the passenger seat of his boat, hoping to battle an oversize fish.

The 350 Chevy in the 21-foot jet boat beat with authority as we idled away from the ramp. For once the Columbia was calm.

Jon Lewis eased the boat away from the rocks and opened up the throttle as we cut the mirror surface under leaden skies.

I watched the fish finder with curiosity for the little blips that might mean we were passing over sturgeon at depths of 35 to 40 feet. But we weren't using the fish finder to locate our fish. Today the fish would come to us.

We dropped anchor in 20 feet of water then Jon threw out sea anchors to hold us in position.

Today, oversize fish were the target. And big fish require big baits. We would use three- and four-pound shad, stringing them whole on 132-pound test leader knotted to 9/0 hooks. For weight, we employed 12-ounce pyramid sinkers.

Sturgeon feed upriver. They use their sense of smell to guide them to the shellfish and decaying matter that they feed upon. So we rigged the shad to point down river with the hook in its mouth.

A good bait is one that has started to come apart. Jon slices the shad then injects it with scent. He explained that it usually takes about 45 minutes for the fish to come in to the bait. Then the action will be steady.

Line peeled off that big Shimano bait-casting reel on the initial run. Jon threw the anchor buoy over the side and cut us loose as the fish blasted away. I tightened down the drag and the fish began to pull the boat. Upstream. Then she turned, circling us. We followed her to the bow and

Above: Mike cradles a nice keeper sturgeon before sending it back to the river. Photo courtesy Outdoors NW

then around the other side of the boat as she went under us and headed back to the anchor rope. I felt the line hit the rope and then horsed her back before she could get tangled in it.

Though we were free of the anchor, the river didn't take us downstream because the fish didn't want to go, running first toward the Oregon shore, then toward Washington. After thirty minutes, she came to the surface and we got our first look at her.

We decided to beach the fish on the Washington side, revive her in the water, and let her go. She would have none of it. I could not bring her into the shallows. Twice we beached the boat and got out. Twice we climbed back in and followed the great fish.

The line was frayed now from chafing on the rocky ledges. Still, I put the backbone of the rod into the fight, though my back ached and my arms were sore. It was the only way to get the fish alongside. Finally, we could see her great head appearing in the green water. Jon reached down and held the fish while I set the rod aside and grabbed the tail, measuring her alongside the boat. Then Jon slipped the hook out and let her kick away into the deep water.

I was holding the tape measure, reading the tale it told and had to look again to make sure I was reading it right. Eight feet, seven inches long.

Over 20 subspecies of sturgeon are found in oceans, some lakes, and a few rivers throughout the Northern Hemisphere. There are seven subspecies in the United States. Europe's Beluga is the largest, sometimes tipping the scales over 3000 pounds. They have been called the ugliest fish on the planet, but beauty is in the eye of the beholder. Maybe a sturgeon wouldn't win any beauty contests, but after a long battle, the sight of one is enough to put a thrill into any angler's heart.

Sturgeon have a skeleton composed of cartilage with a tail similar to that of a shark. A single dorsal fin is set just ahead of the anal fin. The long, rounded body is studded with raised, horny plates called scutes. Their long snout has four barbels in front of a protractile mouth made for vacuuming tasties from the bottom of the river.

Green sturgeon (*Acipenser medirostris*) are rarely found in freshwater. Their saltwater habitat extends from California north to Alaska. Olive-green in color with a stripe running the length of its side and another on the belly, a green is smaller than a white sturgeon. Its flesh is scorned by most.

The meat of the white sturgeon, on the other hand, is highly-prized and that has contributed to its decline in the Northwest. Over-harvest in the late 1800s and early 1900s reduced the number of fish in Oregon and Washington. Still, Columbia River sturgeon provide great sport for many anglers every year.

White sturgeon (*Acipenser transmontanus*) are paler in color than other sturgeon, steel-gray on the back and white on the belly. The snout is short and broad with barbels located in front of the mouth.

White sturgeon travel far upriver following food sources and the urge to spawn. Besides the Columbia, they can be found in the Umpqua, Snake, Willamette, and other rivers. Sturgeon fisheries exist in Tillamook Bay and Willapa Bay. In the upper Columbia they have become landlocked by the construction of dams. Fish ladders are designed for steelhead and salmon. Because of its size, it is extremely difficult for a sturgeon to negotiate a fish ladder.

Sturgeon can live for more than 100 years and may reach lengths exceeding 15 feet. One fish, taken by gill net, tipped the scales at 1285 pounds. A Fraser River sturgeon weighed 1800 pounds. As with many other species of fish, the largest ones are females. These large females are valued spawners and, when hooked, should be played and released quickly. One large female that was caught and killed was said to have carried 250 pounds of eggs.

They reach sexual maturity at 14 years (about 50 inches long) and females will spawn every three to five years. There may be a million sturgeon between Bonneville Dam and the ocean, but only a small percentage, approximately 10,000, make up the spawning population.

The sturgeon spawn is controlled by water temperature and occurs when the temperature averages between 50 and 63 degrees. Sturgeon spawn in swift water over rocks and gravel, broadcasting the eggs. The fertilized egg attaches to gravel or whatever else it comes in contact with. Microscopic plankton supports the young sturgeon as they grow.

The first month of a sturgeon's life it can grow to just over an inch and a half long. As they reach six inches in length, their diet changes and they begin to devour algae, insect larvae and other larger organisms. The young sturgeon may be as long as twelve inches by the end of its first year. Where a sturgeon lives makes a

difference to how big the fish will get. In the Columbia, landlocked fish don't grow as fast as downriver fish.

Because of the disparity in food available it is difficult to estimate with certainty how old a fish is based on its size. Instead, biologists take a slice of a fish's fin to determine its age, much like the way trees are aged by counting annual rings. Still, an angler can make an educated guess about a sturgeon's age by using a tape measure.

A 30-inch "shaker" is a seven year-old fish. At 42 inches, a sturgeon is probably in its 11th year. A 60-inch fish is approximately 18 years of age. A six-footer is a 24 year-old. The eight-foot sturgeon that takes over an hour to come to the boat, has probably just passed the 45-year mark. Should you be fortunate enough to tangle with a nine-footer, play her gentle and release her quickly, that grandmother is nearly 80 years old!

Columbia River sturgeon fishing is regulated by Oregon and Washington. A strict slot limit keeps anglers from harvesting too many young fish and from harvesting any old fish. Anglers are allowed to kill ten "keeper" sturgeon per year. The slot limit ensures that the biggest fish (productive female spawners) are left in the river to perpetuate the species.

The trouble with a slot limit is that the legal-size sturgeon are vulnerable to anglers for several years, until they grow beyond the legal retention range. Not enough of these fish are allowed to grow old and productive. If you don't need to kill a sturgeon, let it go.

Chuck Polityka, a former US government fisheries biologist and water-quality expert, has been guiding sturgeon fishermen on the Columbia for seven years. He operates Outdoors NW Fishing Service and specializes on the Columbia River between Bonneville Dam and Longview.

He is a devoted student of the sturgeon and feels a responsibility toward the fishery upon which he makes his living. He agreed to share his knowledge with the readers of this book to encourage an appreciation of the sturgeon as more than merely a sport fish. Much of the information in this chapter comes from his knowledge and experience.

Sturgeon are opportunistic bottom feeders that follow the feed, rooting with their snouts and detecting morsels with their sensitive barbels. Find the feed and you will find the fish. Contrary to common belief, a sturgeon's eyesight is sharp, though it relies mainly on its excellent sense of smell to find a meal. Sturgeon have been known to eat corn, wheat, onions and other produce that spills from barges on the way downriver.

Freshwater clams, decaying flesh, lamprey larva, eggs, worms, crayfish, snails, and anything else that lives, grows, and dies on the bottom can be food for sturgeon. Columbia River fish travel up and down the river to find the best concentrations of food.

Little depressions in the river bottom concentrate the food as the current sweeps it downstream. A depth finder helps the fisherman find these hidden sturgeon kitchens. Look for places where the depth changes, little depressions ten to twenty feet deeper than the surrounding bottom. The exception is when sturgeon are feeding on clams which are usually found in flat beds. Find freshwater clams, says Polityka, and you will find fish there, year after year.

Food also collects at the edges of drop-offs. Don't ignore these spots when you locate them with your fish finder. Food gathers in front of- and in the eddies behind jetties, islands, tributaries, yacht clubs, and grain elevators.

When your depth finder locates the kitchen, look for the fish, then set up upstream to run your lines back to them. Often the fish finder will show other fish higher in the water column. Because of their smaller air bladders, sturgeon are harder to spot. Look for blips along the bottom. Use the zoom feature on your depth finder to magnify the bottom.

In the winter, sturgeon target freshwater clam beds, baby lamprey, decaying salmon and steelhead flesh, and dead juvenile shad. Decaying fish can be found at any time of year, but it pays to know what is happening with other fish species throughout the year.

Springtime means smelt, a sturgeon favorite, can be found in the Columbia and tributaries. A 50-inch, 58-pound sturgeon was found to have 109 smelt in its stomach.

Shortly after the smelt run, lampreys enter the river to spawn. Sturgeon catch live lamprey or eat the dead ones after they spawn.

In May, June and July, shad are running upstream. A large percentage of shad die after spawning and become sturgeon feed through the rest of the summer.

Sturgeon are strong swimmers and can chase down and eat live baitfish. At the mouths of streams with hatchery programs, sturgeon feed on escaped and released fingerlings. Dead fish, though, make up the bulk of their diet. Dam turbines kill many fish. Opportunistic feeders, sturgeon, line up in the tailrace to cash in on the carnage.

The movement of sturgeon up and down the Columbia River is directly related to spawning urges and available food. Between May and September, the best fishing for keeper-size fish is in the estuary. At that time, bigger fish are moving upstream to spawn. There are always sturgeon in any section of the river at any time of the year.

Choose your bait to match the predominant food the fish are eating. A good sturgeon fisherman is flexible. Try different bait combinations on as many rods as possible to find the most irresistible. If four fishermen are side by side, they should each fish different baits to find which will produce the most action. Polityka might fish one rod with a smelt bait, another with a squid, another with eel, and another with a sand shrimp.

Water temperature has a great impact on the fish and fishing. Polityka recommends using smaller baits when water temperature is lower. Go lighter in leader at the same time to lower the resistance and drag. The lower temperature causes the fish to move slower and to eat less.

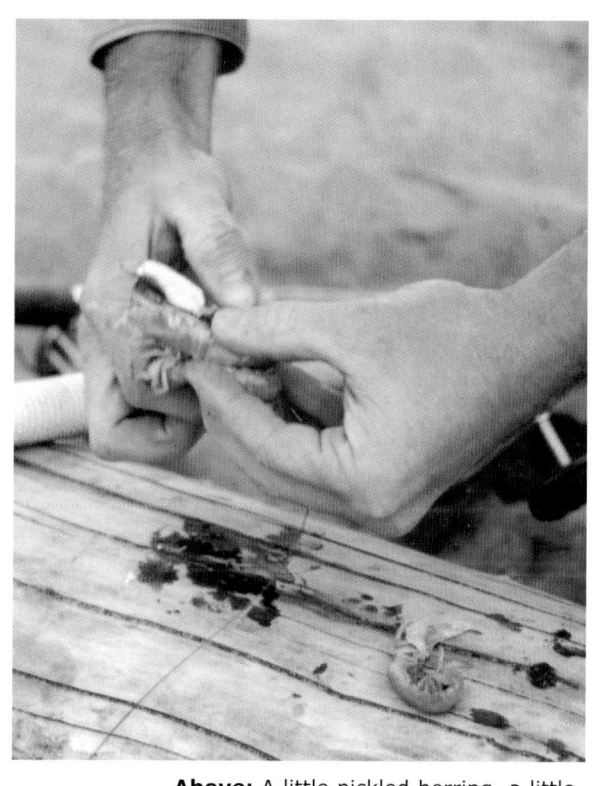

Above: A little pickled herring, a little sandshrimp. Shannon Winters prepares a sturgeon bait. Photo by Gary Lewis

RIGGING

The most important part of your tackle is the hook. Fishing regulations on the Columbia River require a barbless hook to facilitate a quick release. According to Polityka, there should be no place in your sturgeon tackle box for plated hooks. Instead, you want a hook that will, if broken off in a fish's mouth, deteriorate quickly. Use a 5/0-9/0 barbless single hook, tied on Dacron leaders. When fishing for oversize fish, use a 9/0-11/0 hook. Tie up leaders in advance for quick replacement on the river. Leave the leader long until it is rigged with bait. When rigged, best leader lengths for sturgeon are six to fourteen inches, unless you're using whole shad for bait. When fishing with whole shad, use a longer leader. Leader length depends on the type and size of bait being used as well as how it is rigged. Use a longer leader if you half-hitch the bait and shorter if you thread the bait.

Use a sliding sinker rig to allow the fish to take the bait without feeling much resistance from the weight, but heavy enough to keep your bait on the bottom. This will change based on current and tidal influence. Sinkers should be rigged to slide freely on the line using plastic tubing to protect your main line. Keep a selection of sinkers from 4-to 48-ounce.

The main line for fishing for "keeper" fish should be between 30 and 40 pound test. Most anglers use a non-stretch braided line. Bank anglers often choose monofilament because it offers better abrasion resistance. Braided line is a good choice for the boat angler because it doesn't stretch and allows a quick hook set. Go to heavier line when fishing for oversize fish.

Carry a selection of scents in sealed bags and plastic containers. Garlic, Shad, Crawdad, Shrimp, WD40 and others will give you the ability to customize your baits, hopefully making them more tantalizing to fish. The more scents you carry in your sturgeon gear, the more flexibility you have.

BANK FISHING

A sturdy nine- to twelve-foot rod rigged with 40- to 80-pound line is a good setup for the bank fisherman. The rod should have a light tip for sensitivity and a heavy butt for control. A heavy-duty reel of good quality will allow you to handle large fish and cast heavy sinkers. Most fishermen lean toward bait-casting reels, but large spinning reels can do the job.

Since sturgeon use their sense of smell to find food, it might be some time before fish move in to the bait. Polityka emphasizes that a good scent trail is important to successful sturgeon fishing.

BOAT FISHING

Boat fishing requires different tackle and techniques. As a fishing guide Chuck Polityka has very definite ideas on boat fishing. Safety is of the utmost importance. Follow a few simple safety rules and you may save life and limb among the anglers on your boat.

The Columbia River is a river that has been tamed, turned into a highway for heavy commercial traffic. It is controlled by dams, used to generate electricity, and provide food. It is also a playground for water skiers, hunters, fishermen and pleasure boaters. But beneath its benign exterior beats the heart of a beast. This river can kill you. Deep, strong currents called undertows can pull you down and keep you down. High winds can whip up whitecaps that can swamp a small boat or beat your craft to pieces on a jetty. Sandbars that can destroy your outboard prop lurk beneath the surface in the middle of the river. Drifting debris can eviscerate your boat or destroy your motor. And a tugboat pushing a barge can crush your boat beneath its prow. Those are just a few of the ways that the river can kill. Don't help it by operating a boat under the influence of alcohol.

Learn where the navigable channel is so you don't run aground in shallow water. Learn to recognize navigational aids such as red and green buoys, range markers and the five-blast danger signal from a vessel bearing down on you. See the Oregon Boater's Handbook for more information.

Setting anchor and pulling anchor are operations fraught with danger in a river as powerful and prone to change as is the Columbia. Old pilings, submerged cars, floating timber, old fish nets and many other hazards lurk beneath the surface. Commercial traffic, changing tides and varying water levels are all factors you must deal with, each time you boat on the Columbia. When at anchor be on the lookout for floating debris that may come down on your anchor line. Be alert, be safe.

The casual sturgeon fisherman can get by with one boat rod. A seven-foot rod is a good length for a boat rod. Polityka uses three types of rods, based on water conditions and whether small baits or large baits are being used. For light tackle situations, use a seven-foot rod rated for 20- to 50-pound test line. The rod should have a firm backbone, but a soft tip. Polityka uses a Penn 310 GTI reel (or equivalent) with 50- to 65-pound Tuf Plus line.

Use a medium-action rod rated for 50-pound line when pursuing "keeper" fish. 65-pound mainline spun on a Penn 320 GTI (or equivalent) is a good match.

When pursuing oversize fish, use a heavier rod rated 30 to 80 pounds. You need a bigger reel to handle heavier line and a good drag setup to stand up to long runs. The Daiwa 400H and Newell 447 (and equivalents) are good choices, loaded with 80-pound Tuf Plus.

When setting up your boat with the gear to chase sturgeon for the first time, consider booking a trip with a guide first. Some guides will ride with you, on your own boat, to show you how to use your new equipment the right way.

THE BITE

The bite is depends on the type of bait, the temperature of the water, the size of the fish and many other factors. Most anglers leave the rod in the rod holder, watching the tip until the take is real. A fish might worry the bait, smelling it, tasting it, nibbling it. Crayfish, sculpin, peamouth and other fish might work on it, but not if sturgeon are around. Eventually, the sturgeon will decide he wants it. If it is a fish bait, he will turn it in order to eat the fish head first. For that reason the bait should be presented with the head downstream so the fish can pick it up easily and swallow it.

When the water temperature is in the low 40s and 50s expect a subtle bite. When the water is cool and the current is heavy, you have to fight both the fish's lethargy and the river. Put that bait right on their nose in such situations. You may have to move the boat in order to go to the fish because they may not want to come to you. As water temperature increases, the bite will be more pronounced.

Suddenly, the bite will change. You will see it in the tip. SLOWLY lift the rod. TRY NOT TO MOVE THE BAIT. If you can feel resistance - set the hook!. Or, lift the rod slowly, gently, and take up the slack with the reel. Feel the weight of the fish - set the hook. Sometimes, though, the fish takes it fast, swallows the bait and runs with it, slamming the rod down. Hold on.

Now the sturgeon knows he is hooked. Something is wrong with this bait he just ate. He shakes his head and starts to run.

THE FIGHT

A smaller fish is easily brought to hand in a few minutes. It will run several times and it may jump. A bigger fish will take longer and may require every fiber in your being to subdue. Eight-foot sturgeon can tow a jet sled upriver. It may jump multiple times. There is no greater freshwater angling thrill than seeing an eight-foot dinosaur clear the water.

When Polityka hooks one of these monster fish, he implements a game plan to bring the sturgeon safely to the boat. Polityka says that good housekeeping and a game plan that his passengers understand and carry out helps him keep his boat (and passengers) safe. The boat operator and the fisherman are equal partners in the battle, seeking to bring the fish in as soon as possible.

He brings the sea anchors (a.k.a. drag bags) in. All other lines are quickly reeled in. Anglers catch the weights as they come out of the water and remove the weights so that a swinging sinker doesn't injure a passenger. Rods are stowed below the gunwales to prevent breakage. The anchor rope is left on a buoy while the boat drifts with the fish. A quadrant is cleared, allowing the fisherman to fight the fish from one section of the boat without interference from others. At this point, Polityka uses a trolling motor to stay with the fish.

Photo courtesy Outdoors NW

When fighting a big sturgeon, he works hard to bring it to the boat as quickly as possible so that excessive lactic acid buildup in the sturgeon doesn't poison it.

THE RELEASE

Because the stress of battle causes an increase of toxic lactic acid in the sturgeon, the longer the fight, the higher the chance the fish will die of its own poison. For this reason, it is important to release the fish quickly. Barbless hooks make catch and release easier. With "shakers" and "keepers" leave the fish in the water until the cameraman is ready. Lift it high, smile, and return it to the water. Slip the hook out. If the fish swallowed the hook, don't try to remove it by pulling on the line. Instead, cut the line as close to the hook as possible. Excessive leader length will damage the fish's intestines. The hook will rapidly dissolve as long as you aren't using plated hooks.

After you have removed the hook, cradle the fish and rock it slowly, working water through the gill plates. Let it go when it makes a strong kick and pushes away.

It is illegal to remove any part of an oversize fish from the water. Roll the fish on its back and it will calm down. Hold it by the lips while you remove the hook. Now would be the time to take photos. Roll the fish over and revive it by rocking the fish back and forth slowly until it kicks away under its own power. High fives all around.

A final word: Sturgeon fishing regulations are in a constant state of evolution as scientists, fisheries managers, and fishermen learn more about these great fish. Take the time to read the current regulations before you fish.

LARGEMOUTH BASS

This eastern Oregon largemouth hit a crankbait.
Gary Lewis photo

Above: Robert Johansen displays a five-pound largemouth he boated on Washington's Silver Lake.
Photo by Robert Johansen

In the early afternoon there were no clouds in the desert sky and little wind to fight the canoe. We paddled into an inlet arm, passing rocky outcroppings, working our way back to where a small stream fed the reservoir. Sagebrush and juniper trees grew down to the water's edge. Shale slides and tumbled boulders created varied structure points and shallow bays. Juniper stumps were visible beneath the surface.

Jim Johnson was using ultra-light tackle: a five-foot spinning rod, four-pound Maxima and a smoky-metalflake grub. I tied on a Luhr Jensen Speed Trap Crankbait, designed to run in three to fifteen feet of water.

When we spotted the bass, they were in a shallow, weedy flat at the head of the inlet. They ran for deep water when they saw us. We backed up and Jim worked the edge of a rock wall in ten feet of water, bouncing his grub along the bottom. I took the opportunity to check the water temperature.

Early in the spring, water temperatures climb and the fish activity rises as their metabolism awakens from the doldrums of winter. While water temperatures increase from the mid-40's to the mid-50's, largemouth bass can be found feeding in two to fifteen feet of water.

Water temperatures vary in any body of water. Springs and feeder creeks often supply cooler water. Shallow bays usually run warmer than deep, dark water. Fish gravitate to the temperatures where they are most comfortable and seek out shallows where plant and insect life are more abundant.

Water temperatures are the key to bass fishing

In April and early May, look for bass along the shoreline, prowling the shallows adjacent to deep water. Medium-running crank baits, worms, light jigs, spinner baits, and sinking minnow imitations are good choices at these depths. As temperatures hit the mid-50's bass turn aggressive.

Close to the surface, the thermometer read 56 degrees. If we hadn't spooked them already, we should be able to catch a few, I guessed. Jim hooked a fish. His rod bent over in a fierce arc and the light tip shivered as the fish pulled line off the reel. Soon he had it at the boat and reached to grab it by the lower lip, holding it up for me to take a look. I put the thermometer away. I had some catching up to do.

Jim caught the next one as well, while I fooled around stripping plant life from my hooks. When we paddled away from the weedy shallows, my luck changed. The most strikes came from shallow bays between rocky outcroppings. Many times the fish were less than two feet from the bank, striking my crankbait on the first or second turn of the reel.

Other times, in deeper water, a fish would grab the lure as it dug down toward the bottom. Jim found his best success by casting, letting the grub drop and flutter, then pulling it back to him by raising the rod tip and reeling down in a jigging retrieve.

When the bite slowed, we headed for the main lake again, casting to the bank and retrieving. Other times we nosed into the bank and cast lengthwise along the beach, bringing our lures back along the weedbeds or drowned juniper trees.

Above: Brent Shores fished Owyhee Reservoir in July and caught several nice bass on a Strike King series 6 crankbait and an Exude 6-1/2 inch lizard. Photo courtesy Brent Shores.

The key to bass fishing is structure. Stumps, downed trees, docks, weedbeds and rocky outcroppings attract baitfish, which in turn attract bass. The bass find safety from ospreys and other predators in the shadow of the structure and find food in the schools of baitfish.

You can often judge the depth and character of the water in a reservoir by looking at the surrounding terrain. Finger ridges continue to run under water. Steep hills mean sharply changing depths, while flat ground, running into the water, indicates shallows.

Working along the south edge of the lake, we spotted an old dock, half submerged. My cast went long, but it struck the dock and bounced into the water. Before I could turn my reel, a bass had nailed the crankbait. I brought the strong-running fish alongside the boat, reached down and twisted the hook out.

When I was 19, I was fortunate enough to have two farm ponds within walking distance of the house. One was a two-acre impoundment surrounded by willows and the other was smaller, less than half an acre in size and protected by blackberries, willows and a few tall firs.

The smaller pond was my favorite. I discovered an old boat stuck in the weeds. Bailing it out, I pressed it back into service, using a stout pole for propulsion. It was really just the shell of an old drift boat, it leaked a little, but the silt in the bottom kept most of the holes plugged. There were no seats so I had to stand.

The pond was narrow and shallow on one end, deep and wide at the other. The boat allowed me to reach every spot on the pond and gave me room to back-cast when I chose to bring the fly rod.

I remember one fish in particular. I was fishing a purple worm, rigged with a weedless hook and a bullet sinker. I poled the boat into position and made my first cast to the shoreline. I had overthrown the worm. As it sailed to the bank, I stopped it in mid-air and it dropped with a plop right at the waterline.

The fish took it before I had time to crank the reel one revolution, swirling at the bank, jumping at the taste of the steel. She was a two-pound female and she taught me that I could catch fish inches from shore. In the days that followed, I caught a number of bass in that very spot, sneaking up on them from over the rim of the dike, casting a worm or spinner bait to the shallow trough at the edge of the trees.

There are two reasons why spring fishing for bass can be so fun. First, rising temperatures have raised the metabolism of these warm-water fish and so they are hungry. Second, bass spawn in the spring. If you want to catch a big one, your chances are best when females are heavy with eggs.

Having fed little over the winter, bass are on the prowl in the spring, feeding aggressively and, in the case of big females, cruising the shallows, thinking about nesting.

Bass spawn in the spring, typically when water temperatures hit 60 degrees. The pre-spawn is one of the best times of the year to catch big bass as they throw some of their caution aside in favor of bulking up after a long winter.

In most cases, small ponds warm faster than larger lakes and reservoirs so fishing picks up in the smaller waters first. Early in the season, the northeast side of a pond or a point is a good place to prospect for bass. These spots get the most afternoon sunlight.

In larger bodies of water, look to the shallows and the places where ridges point into the water. If there are rocks, drowned trees or other structure, so much the better. Big bass set up in these spots to ambush smaller fish funneling past as they follow the drop-off.

I caught my biggest largemouth bass in the larger pond in early May. I was testing a new five and a half-foot ultralight rod that my uncle had built for

me. I cast a floating perch-pattern Rapala under an overhanging willow and promptly tangled the line at the reel.

As I pulled the loop off the spool, I made the plug skitter in the water and a big bass thrashed it. I was able to get the line back on the reel and crank the fish in after a long battle. With that big bass finally on the bank I knew I was finished rod testing for the day. I wanted to get her on the scales. She weighed a little over five pounds.

Floating minnowbaits, rubber worms, spinners and buzzbaits all make good early season lures for spring bass. Fish the minnowbaits like a topwater lure, using the twitch and pause technique, or simply cast and retrieve. Rubber worms are best fished slow-crawled over structure. Vary retrieves for spinners and buzzbaits, fishing deep and slow or fast and bulging the surface.

Spring bass fishing, when the weather is warm, can be as good as it gets. And it always beats yard work.

In early summer, the fishing can go from tough one day to fantastic the next. Post-spawn fish are still recovering from the rigors of pro-creation. As water temperatures continue to rise, you may find some of the best fly fishing of the year.

The sun was coloring the western clouds in pink and orange even though the day's heat was still in the

Above: When you spot a feeding bass, don't cast directly to it or beyond it. Bass like to chase their food. Cast six feet or more ahead of the fish and watch what happens.

dust and the sage. The wind blew whispers in the grass. Dragonflies flitted across the surface of the water and clung to the shoreside willows.

These willows provided the only cover for the bass. I knotted a large baitfish pattern to my six-pound tippet and cast along the shallows, just out from the brush.

The fly sank and I began my retrieve: a series of three six-inch strips punctuated by a pause. A fish bulged behind the fly. I stripped again and hooked it. The largemouth put a good bend in my eight-weight rod before throwing the hook. I waited a few minutes and tried again, hooking another on the third cast.

This fish was not as big as the first one I had hooked, but it came to the surface in the same way. Shattering the stillness, tailwalking in a spray of water, its mouth gaped wide as it tried to throw the hook. It made a couple of short runs before I hefted the one-pound largemouth out of the water. Unhooking it, I watched it kick away from shore, seeking safety in the deep water of the farm pond.

Rising water temperatures can trigger bass feeding frenzies. The key to finding the fish lies in understanding behavior. Bass are warmwater fish. In the spring they seek the shallows where the sun has the most effect on the water. And, as any stillwater trout fisherman knows, food is also more abundant in the shallows.

When flyrodding for bass, I like sculpin imitations, the deer hair mouserat and dragonfly patterns. Later in the season, large poppers, long rabbit hair streamers and crayfish patterns will be effective.

Use polarized glasses when fishing for bass in the shallows. Often you can see them in less than two feet of water. When you look, don't expect to see the fish, expect to see parts of the fish. Look for an olive back against the bottom or the black end of its tail.

When fishing gear in shallow water to three feet deep, the best choices are stick baits (minnow imitations), spinner baits, buzz baits, shallow crankbaits, and plastic worms without weight.

Use cover to break up your outline when fishing to spooky bass. Hide

Fishing Minnow Imitations

There are few things more exciting than seeing the open maw of a big aggressive largemouth eat your lure on or near the surface. Warm mornings and evenings are the best time to catch largemouth bass on a floating minnow imitation. Cast to cruising fish or prospect near overhanging brush.

Smaller lures will elicit more strikes, but larger baits will help you target bigger fish. Always try to match the size and color of your minnow imitation to forage fish present in the lake. Fish near the surface can see the angler easier than deeper fish. Keep a low profile to lower the chances of spooking wary bass.

Vary the retrieve to find the speed and action that triggers the most strikes. Cast and crank. If that doesn't work, drop your tip to the water and waggle the rod as you reel. A slow twitch-pause retrieve can provoke stubborn fish into striking.

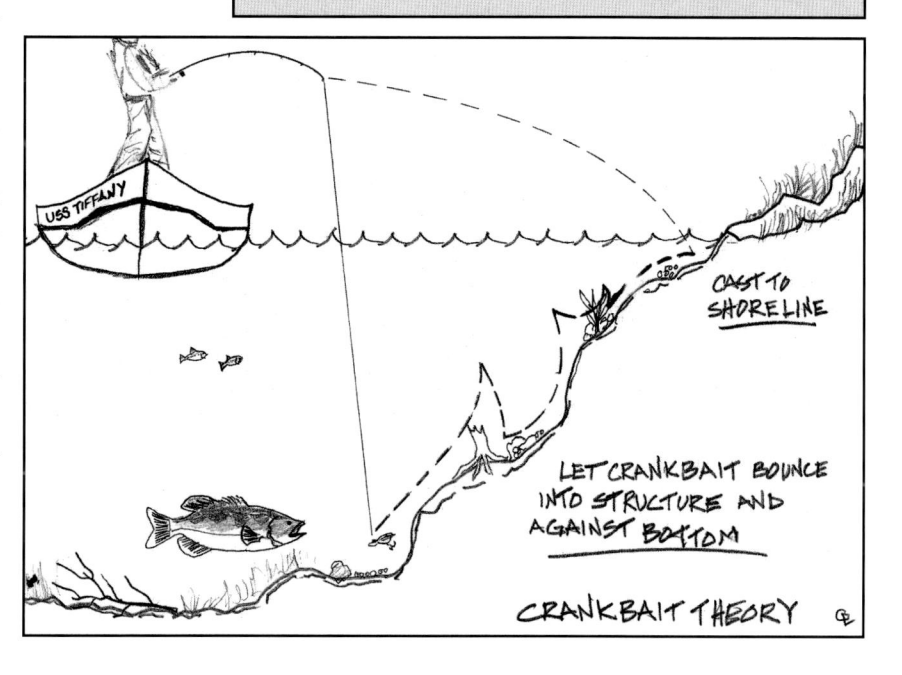

CRANKBAIT THEORY

behind bushes or below the dam on a farm pond. Remember, if you can see the fish, they can see you.

When you spot a feeding bass, don't cast directly to it or beyond it. Bass like to chase their food. Cast six feet or more ahead of the fish and watch what happens.

Bass are seldom very far from some kind of cover. Submerged trees, grass, willows and ledges provide the structure that bass need to conceal themselves from predators. Since baitfish seek the same kind of shelter, bass can find food there as well.

If there are bass close by but you can't get them to take your lure, mix it up a little. Keep trying different lures and retrieves until you find a combination that works. Going back through my journals, summer baits that work best for me are rubber

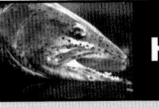

How to Fish Spinner Baits

Submerged trees, grass, willows and ledges provide the structure that bass need to conceal themselves from predators. Since baitfish seek the same kind of shelter, bass can find food there as well.

In summer, you will find bass moving to deeper water as the sun climbs to midday. One of the most effective summer bass lures is the spinner bait. Fish your spinner bait slower and deeper when the sun is high. In the evenings, bass will be found in shallow water again.

For best results, try several different techniques. Cast and retrieve, keeping the lure within five feet of the surface. If the sun is high, try a slow, bottom-bouncing retrieve. Be sure to tick the lure on rocks and roll it over sunken logs and other structure.

When the sun is concealed or is low on the horizon, try a bulging retrieve. Reel fast enough to keep the lure close to the surface, leaving a visible wake behind it. Bass may also take a jigged spinner bait. Cast into bass-holding cover, let the lure fall to the bottom, then lift and let it fall again, retrieving slowly.

worms retrieved painfully slow, topwater plugs, crankbaits, and flies.

If you are fishing from a boat, cast right to the bank and be ready to set the hook the moment your lure hits the water. Shallow water bass are very aware of what is moving above them. I've seen bass key on the lure while it is still in the air, streak from fifteen feet away, and catch it as it hits the water.

Largemouth bass change their habits as the water warms from the mid-60's to the 70's. You will find bass near the surface in the morning, moving deeper as the sun climbs to midday. In the evenings, bass will be found in shallow water again.

Clear, calm water makes bass feel vulnerable to predators from above. Herons, kingfishers, ospreys and humans, among others are all eager to make a meal out of a bass. A wise old bass who doesn't want to accept an invitation to dinner, stays deep when the sun is high, the water is calm, and the sky is clear.

When fishing in three to ten feet of water, use medium-running crank baits, worms, light jigs, spinner baits, and sinking minnow imitations.

On overcast summer days you may find bass feeding near the surface during the middle of the afternoon.

I fished one such day in mid-July and stood in the leaky boat, working line through the guides. The huge mouserat fly was awkward to cast but I managed to set it down with a splash under the overhanging trees,

Above: Trevor Mayfield landed this big largemouth at Prineville Reservoir in October. Photo courtesy Rod Mayfield, Moonlight Marine

right next to the bank. I swam it back to me, moving the rod tip from side to side, twisting the line with my left hand as I slowly retrieved.

The surface was shattered as a largemouth bass engulfed the mouse. The first of many to fall to the mouse that day. From that point forward there has always been a hole for a mouse in my fly box.

As the days get shorter and the nights are getting long, the bass feel like they're running out of time. This can spark feeding activity as the bass bulk up for the winter. On warm, sunny autumn days, you may find the fish in the same places you found them in the pre-spawn. The water temperature is going down from the 70's to the 60's. Good fishing can be found in the shallows with good access to deep water. Near points, cliffs and submerged trees, the bass will go vertical along the structure, in deeper water at midday and shallower when the sun is low.

When fishing in ten feet and deeper water, jigs, natural bait, plastic worms, spoons, deep-diving crankbaits and spinner baits are your best bets.

Pinpoint their depth and tune your presentation to match it and you will catch fish.

One fall evening on an old quarry lake that drains into the North Fork of the Lewis River, I found the bass right at the bank. The water was deepest on our side of the lake and the willows hung out over the water. Approaching carefully, I threw a yellow octopus jig beneath the willow tree and was rewarded with a smashing strike. My friend Mike Tom and I fished until dark, catching bass on jigs then switched to spinnerbaits retrieved so fast that the surface bulged with speed of the lure and the chasing bass. We quit fishing when it was too dark to see.

In the winter, bass are living deep. You can still catch a bass in December, January and February but it requires a change in tactics. Fish low and slow. One February, the weather was so cold that every body of water around had ice over it, except the swiftest parts of the rivers. Sometimes you just have to go fishing.

My brother-in-law, Shannon Winters, from Woodland Washington, joined me in an ice-fishing adventure on a small farm pond. Could a warmwater fish bite in sub-freezing temperatures? We would find out or get frostbitten in the process.

The ice supported our weight. In fact, it was so thick that I could have driven my car on it. Nevertheless, we chopped a hole over the deepest part of the pond and lowered our baits. We hunched over our rods, husbanding our energy, seeking to keep what little heat was in our bodies from escaping.

A fish took my bait. I saw the line move and felt an almost imperceptible tug. Lifting my rod, I felt the fish. It kicked once and then I reeled it in, bringing it up on the ice to admire. It was a fine bass, a fish that would have made my heart race with excitement, running and jumping in a gill-rattling display on any warm summer evening. In the dead of winter, it could barely manage a flop. I cradled it gently and let it swim away. I had to catch a fish, but I didn't have to catch anymore. If it was that hard on the bass, I could afford to let them wait out the winter without harassment from me.

Bass can be caught in the winter, but their metabolism dictates that you fish deep and fish slow.

SMALLMOUTH BASS

Above: A John Day River smallmouth bass.
Photo by Gary Lewis

Ask any seasoned freshwater fisherman what fish, pound for pound, will give you the hardest battle and you're likely to hear the words 'smallmouth bass.' Known for their tendency to head straight for the surface when hooked, smallmouth will give you a fierce battle on light tackle. Head-shaking runs and a hard fight to the finish is what you get every time you hook one. Best of all, they are curious fish, and are easily taken on a variety of lures and baits.

You don't have to get up early to catch Micropterus dolomieui dolomieui. Nevertheless, when my friend Brian told me to meet him at 4:30 in Redmond, I said okay, setting my alarm for 3:55 a.m.

Morning was pushing back the night when we began the climb into the Ochocos on our way through Mitchell. We headed north along a gravel road, trying to outdo each other spotting game. I saw more deer, while Brian was quicker at spotting antelope, hawks, and golden eagles. The elk were easy to see. We stopped to snap photos and listen to them calling to each other from both sides of the road. This was why we woke early.

Smallmouth are aggressive predators, feeding on smaller fish, insects, leeches, snails, and crayfish

---

We were fishing by 8:00. Here, the river smoothed out in a long, glassy stretch to sweep in a hard right turn downstream, creating a deep pool at the outside of the next bend. A large ponderosa pine was submerged in the deep water.

Upstream, Brian was already standing in the river. He prefers to fish a long-shank No. 1/0 hook tied directly to his main line. Baited with a whole nightcrawler, he can reach most of the water he wants to fish without adding weight. If he can't cast that far, he will wade or swim there.

I caught my first bass of the day on a Luhr Jensen crawdad pattern crankbait. I cast downstream along the submerged tree and cranked it back. The big fish struck hard, putting a deep bend in my spinning rod. It ran downstream, then back toward me, coming to the surface to turn and seek out the bottom again, its bronze flanks flashing in the sun.

Next, it turned to the tree for help, tying the line around the end of a limb. I was stuck. Dropping the rod tip, I saw the line still sawing on the tree. I still had him. After giving him slack for thirty seconds, he pulled the line off the tree and I put the backbone of the rod into it, making sure he didn't tangle up again. At the bank, I admired him, unhooked him and watched him kick away.

For the next few hours, we caught and released more bass than we could count, wading deeper in the cool water as the temperature climbed higher. Worms, crankbaits, jigs, and grubs all caught fish.

Smallmouth bass are not native to the Northwest. They were brought here in buckets by homesick, railroad-traveling easterners. Oregon's best smallmouth fishing can be found in the John Day, Willamette, Umpqua, and Columbia Rivers.

Spawning in the spring, smallmouth bass wait for the water temperature to reach the 60-65 degree range. The male finds a sand/gravel or rocky bottom in a protected spot, such as a next to a boulder or submerged log. He clears away the silt with his tail in

Above: Bob Pengra with a big smallmouth bass.
Photo courtesy Bob Pengra

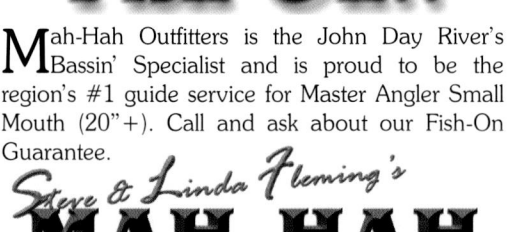

Above: Two on one cast! Photo courtesy Bob Pengra

preparation for the female to move in. The female deposits her eggs and the male fertilizes them and then stays to guard the nest and the hatching fry. It takes about eight years for the smallmouth to reach three pounds. He may live as long as 18 years.

Both largemouths and smallmouths are members of the black bass family. They can be found in the same waters in parts of the Northwest. Largemouth thrive in warmwater lakes, while smallmouth prefer moving water.

Several features set smallmouth apart from largemouth bass. Smallmouth have a jaw extending to below the middle of the eye whereas the largemouth's jaw extends beyond the eye. They are bronze in color (largemouth are olive-colored) and have vertical bars on their flanks. A smallmouth's spiny front dorsal fin is connected to the rear with just a dip in the membrane, rather than the largemouth's notch. Their eyes are sometimes red.

They prefer warm, flowing water in a range of 67 to 71 degrees, and can be found in great numbers around weed beds, grassy banks, along the seams of riffles, deep along rock walls, and in gravel flats. On clear summer days when the sun is high, the biggest fish will be found in deeper water. On overcast days or when the sun is low on the horizon, smallmouth can be caught on or closer to the surface.

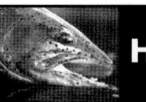

How to Fish Crank Baits

The key to bass fishing is structure. Stumps, downed trees, docks, weedbeds and rocky outcroppings attract baitfish, which in turn attract bass. The bass also find safety from ospreys and other predators in the shadow of the structure.

On warm, sunny days, good fishing can be found in the shallows with access to deep water. Near points, cliffs and submerged trees, the bass will go vertical along the structure. Fish deeper water at midday and shallower when the sun is low.

Crankbaits are made to fish effectively at specific depths from twelve inches deep to twenty feet down. Stock your bass box with a selection of crankbaits to allow you to tailor your presentation to the depth of the fish at any time of the day. Pinpoint the depth of the fish and tune your presentation to match it and you will catch more bass.

They are aggressive predators, feeding on smaller fish, insects, leeches, snails, and crayfish. Since big bass eat little bass, the smaller bass tend to stay in schools away from larger fish. If you are catching little bass, move to deeper water to target larger fish.

Look for bigger bass behind underwater ledges in deep pockets. If there is a mix of broken rocks in those pockets, bass can use those places to ambush smaller fish. Also look for deep water with a sunken tree or old stumps to provide cover for larger bass. Spend the time to fish those spots thoroughly.

Early in the year, as the water temperatures begin to rise, the biggest bass come out of the doldrums first. April and May provide the best opportunities to catch trophy smallmouths. Later in the summer you have to catch a lot of little ones before you hook a lunker.

Bigger fish are not easily caught on the gear that takes the average eight to ten-inch bass. To consistently catch big bass, use big flies and lures. That said, smallmouth are taken on smaller baits than are used for largemouth. They prefer to feed on crayfish along the bottom rather than looking up for their meals. Big bass will look up, though. If small bass are feeding on insects, larger bass will feed on them.

The eyes of a bass are sensitive. In midday, he goes deep to avoid the harsh glare of direct sunlight

---

The eyes of a bass are sensitive. In midday, he goes deep to avoid the harsh glare of direct sunlight. His vision to the front is better than his side vision, but he can see completely around himself. Bass can hear very well and are able to recognize sounds and determine whether a predator is approaching or prey is vulnerable. Sounds that come from the water are picked up through the skin in the inner ears.

The long line from the gill plates to the base of the tail is called a lateral line. He uses his lateral lines to pick up vibrations and follow them to the source of

Right: Early in the year, as the water temperatures begin to rise, the biggest bass come out of the doldrums first. April and May provide the best opportunities to catch trophy smallmouths. Photo courtesy Steve Fleming

the sound. Even in cloudy water he can follow the sounds to the their source.

Smell is very important. The bass's nose is located on its snout between the eyes and the upper lip. It consists of four nostrils. The front nostrils are called the anteriors, and the nostrils closest to the eyes are the posteriors. Water is borne through the anterior nostrils and passes across the olfactory organs before exiting through the posteriors.

The bass tastes his food by nudging it with the outside of his lips. When using a slow retrieve, often the bass will approach the bait and taste it without taking it into his mouth. Such taps are often interpreted by the fisherman as a bite. Set the hook and you are likely to miss, and spook the fish. A faster retrieve will sometimes provoke a strike because the bass doesn't have time to taste. He sees an opportunity for a quick meal and grabs it without tasting it first.

TECHNIQUES AND TACKLE

When targeting smallmouths, a medium-power spinning rig with six- to eight-pound test line is suitable. When fishing bigger water or when the cover is heavier, a bait-casting outfit equipped with ten- to 12-pound line is a better choice.

Deep-running crankbaits are a good choice for targeting bass on the bottom. Another good tactic is dead-drifting a plastic worm, allowing it to tumble through the best holding water. Rig the

Left: Bass are seldom very far from some kind of cover. Submerged trees, grass, willows, and ledges provide the structure that bass need to conceal themselves from predators. Since baitfish seek the same kind of shelter, bass can find food there as well. Photo by Gary Lewis

worm weedless (with hook point buried in the worm) to minimize hooking up on the bottom. Orange and olive crayfish patterns are good crankbait options.

> ### Submerged trees, grass, willows, and ledges provide the structure that bass need to conceal themselves from predators

Plastic worms work well for smallmouth. In shallow water, fish a four-or six-inch worm, unweighted on an ultra-slow retrieve, or fish it weighted with a slip sinker so the fish won't sense the weight on the bite. On the initial strike, drop your rod tip and let the fish take it before setting the hook.

Minnow imitations work very well in smallmouth water, especially along ledges or around submerged structure. Use patterns that imitate local baitfish. Chub, perch, and rainbow patterns work well. Cast and retrieve, holding the rod tip at the surface of the water. Waggle the rod tip to impart action to the lure.

In-line spinners are effective smallmouth lures. Small Rooster Tail, Mepps, and Blue Fox spinners work well. Cast toward structure and retrieve. Don't bring the spinner back in a straight line, though. Move the rod tip from side to side, giving the lure a change of direction every few feet.

Fly anglers should not overlook opportunities to chase black bass with fur and feathers. A seven-weight rod is a good choice for smallmouth waters like the John Day or Umpqua.

Bass feed heavily on aquatic insects in the larval and pupal stages. But don't limit yourself by imitating insects. Bass also chase minnows, crayfish, and terrestrials. Bring patterns to match the biggest bass foods and you will catch more and bigger fish. Start with a weight-forward line, a six-to nine-foot 2x-4x leader and a No. 1-6 fly. Some popular patterns for chasing river bass are the Deer Hair Swimming Frog, Clouser Minnow, Wooly Bugger, Crayfish, Mouserat, Muddler Minnow, and Joe's Hopper.

Use polarized glasses when fishing for bass in rivers. Often you can see them in less than two feet of water. When you look, don't expect to see the fish, expect to see parts of the fish. Look for a bronze-brown back against the bottom or the black end of a tail.

Use streamside cover to break up your outline when fishing to spooky bass. Remember, if you can see the fish, they can see you. When you spot a feeding bass, don't cast directly to it. Bass like to chase their food. Cast six feet or more ahead of the fish and watch what happens.

Bass are seldom very far from some kind of cover. Submerged trees, grass, willows, and ledges provide the structure that bass need to conceal themselves from predators. Since baitfish seek the same kind of shelter, bass can find food there as well.

If you are fishing from a boat, cast to the bank and be ready to set the hook the moment your lure hits the water. Shallow water bass are very aware of what is moving above them.

You can find good bass fishing any time of day, but if you go early you might see the elk or spot a golden eagle on the hunt. Set your alarm clock.

Good fishing for smallmouth bass can be had in places like Washington's Lake Chelan, Banks Lake, Billy Clapp Lake, Mayfield Lake, Lake Washington, Lake Sammamish, Lake Whatcom, Lake Stevens, Palmer Lake, Lake Osoyoos, Moses Lake, and the Potholes Area Seep Lakes. Top smallmouth rivers are the Yakima River, Grand Ronde River, Okanogan River, Snake River, and the Columbia River.

In Oregon, try the mainstem Umpqua River downstream from Roseburg, or head east of the mountains to fish the John Day. Close to Portland, Henry Hagg Lake holds the state record. In Central Oregon, Lake Billy Chinook is home to a good population of smallmouth. Prineville Reservoir has a mixed bag of largemouths and smallmouths. Expect to find smallmouths in the Snake and Columbia River impoundments as well.

STRIPED & HYBRID BASS

STRIPED BASS

The late 1800's were a great time of exploration for sportsmen. Relative peace combined with newfound prosperity and the pioneering spirit sent adventurers in search of new places. When easterners came west they found great new wonders but also found themselves missing their home fields and waters. That is the explanation for many of the northwest's great fisheries. Smallmouth and largemouth bass were introduced in many western rivers by railroad men carrying fish in buckets.

Striped bass were introduced to the west for the same reason. Native to the Atlantic system, the fish was so popular that homesick surf fishermen brought them with them, beginning in 1879. Populations were established in many California rivers and up the coast to the Coos and Umpqua Rivers. The Rogue, Coquille and Alsea have also supported striped bass in the past and may yet harbor remnant runs. At one time there were stripers running in the Columbia River.

Striped bass are named for the six to eight black stripes that line their olive-grayish and silver sides. The back is darker in color, ranging to black and the belly is white. Its tail is forked and it has two separate dorsal fins.

In saltwater, stripers seldom range far from the coast. They feed in bays, in the surf and at the mouths of tributaries and will move into their home rivers to feed in spring and spawn in the fall. In general, they are found in freshwater in the winter, moving out to the salt again when waters begin to warm.

Above: Anna Cheney admires a big striper she caught while fishing the lower Umpqua River. Photo by www.theoregonangler.com

Look for areas with good structure and depth changes, like a point of rocks with sandy beach around it.

The striper prefers fast water over a gravel or sand bottom for spawning. Females, called cows, spawn for the first time in their third or fourth year, weighing between three and six pounds. She will produce upwards of 60,000 eggs that first year and more as she grows. Striped bass can reach 30 pounds and more in size.

In the Umpqua drainage, most stripers spawn in the Smith River. Striper fishermen find success in Winchester Bay using herring, anchovies, smelt and ghost shrimp. Trolling with plugs can also be effective. Fly fishermen do well using large streamer patterns that imitate baitfish. Stripers run in schools of similar sized fish, following the food. Once feeding fish are located, the fishing can be hot

Stripers feed on flounders, squid, eels, shad, crabs, anchovies and pileworms. A single big hook 3/0 to 10/0, rigged through the back or lips of an anchovy and slow-trolled or drifted can be effective. Fish it deep, with a wine cork or similar float to keep it off the bottom.

The best tackle for saltwater stripers is similar to what you would employ for salmon. An eight to nine-foot rod with plenty of backbone, and rigged with 20 to 30 pound test line would be sufficient.

In freshwater or when finesse fishing in the salt, eight-pound test line on a steelhead rod is appropriate. Fish can average four to eight pounds, seldom over fifteen in our northern coast Pacific bass.

Surf fishing can be productive for striped bass. The bass feed on perch in the saltwater and can be caught by anglers targeting both species. As with any surf fishing, the best opportunities are just before, during and after high tide. Good beach fishing for stripers and perch can be found north and south of the mouth of Coos Bay.

Surf fishermen are best served by long, two-handed rods, averaging from ten to twelve feet in length. Good baits are clams, pileworms, squid and baitfish.

Look for areas with good structure and depth changes, like a point of rocks with sandy beach around it.

In the surf, stripers increase their activity while the tide is either rising or falling. Most fishermen seek to place their offering such that the waves will sweep the bait farther out. Enough weight should be used to ensure that the bait is not brought in on the waves.

Hold the rod or place it in a holder to watch for action. You could catch perch or stripers or anything else. Retrieve slowly.

In Oregon, fishing for striped bass is not what it was a few decades ago. The Department of Fish and Wildlife is not likely to seek to enhance this fishery either as big stripers feed on salmon and steelhead smolts. But good fishing can be had on Oregon's southern coast for this exciting sport fish.

For the angler who wants to catch a striper in Oregon, an alternative exists in the high desert.

Left: Todd Hannah hoists a nice striper that fell for a minnow imitation. April and May offer the best fishing for striped bass on the Oregon coast. Photo by www.theoregonangler.com

HYBRID BASS

Hybrid bass are a sterile mixture of striped bass and white bass. They grow larger than white bass and usually live longer than either species. In the northwest they are only available in fishable numbers in one place: Eastern Oregon's Ana Reservoir. Ana Reservoir is a 60-acre reservoir near Summer Lake. Spring-fed, it is ice-free year-round due to the constant influx of 58 degree water.

Also found in Ana Reservoir, are chubs, largemouth bass, and rainbow trout. The hybrids feed on all three. The hybrids have been stocked in the lake since 1982 with additional stockings every other year.

The fish average four to ten pounds. Fifteen-pound hybrids are not unheard-of. Dedicated hybrid bass anglers think the current eighteen-pound, eight-ounce record will be replaced soon.

Best gear for hybrids is a seven to nine foot rod, rigged with a high-capacity spinning reel or casting reel. Eight to fifteen pound test line is appropriate.

Most fishermen employ bait, fishing from the bank. Favorite baits are frozen anchovies, herring, prawns, and chicken liver. The bait should be fished on a sliding sinker so that the fish does not feel the drag as it moves away. When a bass takes the bait, it moves fast, grabbing the bait and running. If it feels the drag of a weight it will expel the bait before the angler can set the hook.

Spinners and spoons are also effective, jigged or retrieved.

Some people fish from a boat, using jigs or trolling plugs. Rainbow or chub pattern minnow-baits or crankbaits have taken hybrids.

Hybrids, like stripers, travel in packs, searching out schools of prey. Experienced hybrid anglers tell of days when the fish go into feeding frenzies. At such times, any bait or lure seems to work.

In the winter and spring, look for deeper water that stays at a constant temperature. As warmer weather raises the water temperature, bass will leave the deep holes and roam the lake on the hunt.

Between feeding binges, solitary fish cruise the edges of underwater shelves, searching for minnows, leeches and other bits of food. Plunking with bait is an effective way to catch these fish which can sometimes be observed through polarized glasses from high on the bank.

In the winter and spring, look for deeper water that stays at a constant temperature. As warmer weather raises the water temperature, bass will leave the deep holes and roam the lake on the hunt.

Hybrid bass are a worthy quarry and one that every Northwest angler wishing to complete his or her angling education should seek out.

TIGER MUSKIES

Above: A big Mayfield Lake tiger muskie. Careful bank anglers can find success by exploring weed beds and structure in shallow bays. Photo by Robert Johansen

Walk softly and carry a heavy rod when you want to tangle with a tiger musky. Because they are equipped with the most ferocious teeth of our freshwater fish, use at least 12 inches of steel leader between your main line and your lure.

Introduced to control rough fish, tiger muskies can be found in a handful of Washington's reservoirs. They are a hatchery-raised hybrid of the northern pike and the muskellunge.

The tiger musky is a long-bodied fish, ferociously handsome with a tall, speckled dorsal fin far at the end of its body. It has a big mouth and a multitude of long, sharp teeth. Its sides are light with camouflaging darker, narrow vertical bars and spots that extend to fins and tail.

These aggressive feeders are not particularly difficult to catch. They feed on squawfish, chubs, trout, bass, perch, and any other fish that they can catch and eat. Frogs, mice, snakes, and ducklings are other targets of opportunity of which a tiger muskie might take advantage.

They may feed during the day or at night. Best opportunities are early in the morning and late in the evening. Weedy areas are the best places to look for tiger muskies. For this reason, careful bank anglers can find success by exploring weed beds and structure in shallow bays. Look for clumps of lily pads, standing timber, submerged stumps, small islands, and beneath boat docks. Anyplace where the big predator can wait in the shade for a meal is a potential place to catch a tiger musky.

Any fish-imitating lure six to 12 inches long is a good place to start. Castaics, Rebels and Rapalas are a good choice. Muskies can also be caught on large bass crankbaits and spinnerbaits. A medium heavy baitcasting outfit with twelve to twenty-pound test monofilament or braided line is a good choice for casting these heavy lures. Always use steel leader.

They are known to follow lures for a long way before striking or, more often, turning away. Boat anglers can easily employ an artifice that is known to provoke strikes. At the end of the retrieve, as the lure approaches the boat, push the rod tip deep into the water and guide the lure in large figure-8s.

As with other predators, changing speed and direction of the lure can also provoke a strike at greater distance from the boat. Try "bulging" the lure at the surface with a fast retrieve or bumping it along the bottom.

If you spot fish and are unable to get them to follow your lure after a few casts, mark their location and go prospecting for other fish. After an hour or two, return and make another try. They are bound to decide to start eating again sometime and you want to be there when it happens.

The State of Washington allows anglers to keep tiger muskies when fish are 36 inches and longer. When Washingtonians talk about muskies, they are usually talking about fishing Mayfield Lake. Mayfield is a reservoir on the Cowlitz River near the town of Mossyrock and was the first place in Washington to receive stocks of tiger muskies.

When I fished Mayfield, we found good musky habitat and fish close to the Mayfield Lake Resort, near the County Park, in the narrows, near the hatchery and in the shallows at Ike Kinswa State Park. There are many other good places to find muskies as well, just look for shallow water, weedy bays and overhead structure.

Other Washington reservoirs that hold tiger muskies include Evergreen Reservoir in Grant County, Merwin Reservoir in Clark County, Curlew Lake in Ferry County, and Newman Lake in Spokane County.

These aggressive feeders are not particularly difficult to catch. They feed on squawfish, chubs, trout, bass, perch, and any other fish that they can catch and eat. Frogs, mice, snakes, and ducklings are other targets of opportunity of which a tiger muskie might take advantage.

Above: Big minnow imitations are the best baits for tiger muskies. Be sure to use a wire leader. Photo by Gary Lewis

Left: Don Johansen with a big tiger muskie from Mayfield Lake. Photo by Robert Johansen

BLUEGILL

Bluegill are a member of the Centrarchidae family, more commonly referred to as sunfish. They can be recognized by the blue-black spot on the edge of the gill plate. They inhabit slow-moving, vegetated water and can be found in the shallows. Many anglers got their start fishing for bluegill before moving on to other species. Many more anglers are still hooked on them.

Bluegill are often caught incidental to the pursuit of other species such as bass or trout, but these scrappy fighters are a worthy challenge in their own right.

They are not native to the Northwest. In the 1890's, the US Fish Commission released bluegill into several eastern Washington lakes. About the same time, bluegill were introduced to the lower Columbia.

Sunfish are often found living in the same waters as largemouth bass. In fact, they are an important part of the largemouth's diet. As a prey species, bluegills spend most of their lives in shallow waters, avoiding the dangers of the deep.

In the spring, when water temperatures reach the upper 60's, bluegill seek out the spawning grounds in approximately three feet of water. Spawning beds can be found in shallow bays with a firm bottom. At this time, the males are easily caught as they jealously guard the nest.

The life span of a bluegill is from five to ten years, but the size of the adult is dependent upon the population of the lake. Sunfish are such prolific breeders that overpopulation, and stunting occurs when predation is light. Where excessive competition for available food occurs, bluegill may average five inches in length. In such places, the best policy is to keep every one you catch, regardless of size. Bluegill average seven to eight inches in length and can grow to twelve inches long.

After a fish has reached sufficient size that a bass is no longer a threat, the bluegill may seek out deeper water, running in schools of similar-sized fish.

The bluegill subsists mainly on insects, snails, and worms. Best fishing times are morning and evening, though bluegill can be caught throughout the day, especially if the sky is overcast.

When targeting bluegills seek out protected, shallow bays that warm quickest in the spring. Submerged grasses are important food sources for bluegill when the water is high. At such times, you can find the fish feeding on the multitude of insects living in the grass.

The branches of underwater trees are another good bet for sunfish. Look for sand or gravel beaches where the lake falls off gradually toward a weed bed. Deep weed beds and deep holes in shallow areas are good places to probe for larger fish. Bluegill may also school and feed in ankle-deep water.

A five to six-foot rod, equipped with a spinning or spin-cast reel and four-pound test line, is optimum for bluegill fishing.

Earthworms are the most popular bait. In the weedy bays where most bluegill are found, the best technique calls for fishing a piece of worm under a float. Other baits that take bluegill readily are mealworms, grasshoppers and crickets. When a suspended bait is not producing, often a turn or two of the reel is all that is necessary to spark the bite.

Bluegill are willing fly tackle opponents as well. On light tackle, they can put up quite a battle. Best fly rod weights for bluegill range from the ultra-light 0 weight to a 5 weight. A floating line is all you will need. Smaller flies are your best bet. Your box should contain poppers, dries, nymphs and wets in sizes 10, 12, 14 and 16.

Silver Lake, Lacamas Lake, Moses Lake, Potholes Reservoir, and Sprague Lake are top producers for bluegill in Washington.

Oregon's best bluegill lakes include Tenmile, Emigrant, Henry Hagg, Mission Creek Reservoir and many more lakes and reservoirs. In addition, countless farm ponds in both states contain good bluegill fishing.

YELLOW PERCH

Our depthfinder indicated that we were anchored in 13 feet of water. The old tailings from the gold dredging operation can be seen along the river channel. Underwater, the mounds of rock and gravel provide structure for the fish. The object, Troy said, was to find a pocket of deep water between tailing piles where the larger trout would hold.

I watched the tip of my rod. Troy was fishing Power Bait out of the other side of the boat while Jim waited to see whose bait would work first.

I felt a tap and saw my rod dip, setting the hook. The fish came toward me at first, then dived back under the boat. A perch. On light tackle, it put up a good fight, but the struggle was quickly over, the fish in the boat.

When we had all boated perch, we moved the boat closer to the tailings in even shallower water. There were plenty of fish to catch and it seemed that wherever we were, whatever we tried, they would take. Most of the fish were in the eight-inch range with a few going larger than that.

We anchored at the mouth of Deer Creek, casting to the brush. I hooked one spiny-rayed perch that really bent the rod, slashing back and forth in the milky water, its olive-barred, yellow flanks flashing in the sun. Reaching down, I swung the fish into the boat and it joined the others in the livewell.

Yellow perch are often overlooked in a region whose fishing is as diverse as ours, yet these fish are well-known in other parts of the country for their willingness to bite, and the taste of their fillets. Yellow perch are often easier caught than other species, because they are more prone to feed in the daylight than other fish.

Wherever perch are found, bank anglers will do well fishing around points, tailing piles, brush or other structure. From boats, many fishermen will anchor in a likely spot and cast spinners or dangle bait beneath the boat. Trollers may hook perch using small Wedding Ring spinners and a bit of worm or shrimp. For perch, a slow troll is best.

I have often caught perch on yellow corn, angleworms, and grubs. Crayfish tails and grasshoppers are other good baits. Artificial lures that work well on these spiny-backed fish are spinners, jigs, wet flies, and streamers. Small baitfish imitations should produce well for yellow perch anglers.

For perch, the best hook size is No. 6 through 10. In deep water, it is best to fish just up from the bottom. From a boat, lower a pyramid sinker to the bottom, with your bait twelve inches above the weight and another dropper positioned a foot above that.

Perch can be caught in shallow water with the standard bobber and worm technique. Suspend your bait so that it is one to two feet from the bottom. Patience should be exercised to avoid pulling the bait away from the fish. The perch will mouth the bait for awhile, positioning it to swallow. Setting the hook too soon won't put many fish on your stringer. Wait until the bobber goes under.

Perch run in groups with other fish of approximately the same size. If the perch you are catching are too small, find another area of the lake if you are looking for something bigger.

Yellow perch are found in some western rivers, but the best fishing is in lakes and ponds. Slow, cool waters with big openings of sand, or gravel bottom make for good perch habitat.

An example is the lower Columbia River, in the stretch from Bonneville down past Kelso. Good perch fishing can be found around jetties, pilings, docks, yacht clubs and grain silos.

Oregon's Henry Hagg Lake and Klamath Lake and Washington's Lacamas Lake in Clark County are examples of good perch water. Big yellow perch can be caught in the Columbia River and Lake Washington. Fish near creek mouths, docks, and shallow flats for good action in the spring and fall. In the heat of summer, the better fishing will be deep or near cold water sources.

CRAPPIE

It was a warm spring day and the sky was white with the high clouds that held the warmth of the day and diffused the sun's light. I poled the boat through the channel against the wind and then let it drift with the breeze along the weed beds.

I slow-trolled a rubber-skirted jig inches away from the grass that grew out of the water. A sharp rap signaled a bite and I set the hook into a sleek, ten-inch crappie, the first of many that I was to catch along that shoreline.

Until that day, I had caught crappie as incidental catches while fishing for bluegills and bass. That was when I began to understand that to consistently catch crappie, you have to target them with specific lures and techniques.

Crappie are a delight to catch and delicious on the table

Two types of crappie, black and white, are found in Washington and Oregon. They use their narrow, deep body to good advantage against a rod, planing in the water. They average eight to twelve inches, though bigger fish can be found. The Oregon State record for black crappie measured 18.5 inches and weighed in at 4 pounds, 6.1 ounces. Oregon's biggest white crappie also measured, 18.5 inches and tipped the scales at 4 pounds, 12 ounces.

Above: Outdoor writer Robert Johansen admires a 14-inch crappie from a Washington lake. Photo by Robert Johansen

Above: This Prineville Reservoir crappie took a grub jigged below a dock. Photo by Gary Lewis

Crappie feed primarily on smaller fish, bugs and crustaceans. Fish of quiet waters, they frequent vegetation that attracts minnows and incubates insects.

When you find one fish you have found many. They are often in large schools and may hold at specific depths around sunken structure. The challenge lies in locating them and plumbing the precise depth where the school is holding.

When conditions are right they are ravenous feeders and come easily to the hook. On other days, they may seem selective and fickle. Stick around, though, and keep experimenting, the right bait can spark the feeding frenzy again.

Rubber skirted jigs are a favorite lure for crappie fishermen. Red and white, and yellow are top producers. Small spinners, small plugs, and spoons also work well. Fly rodders can also get in on the act, casting or trolling small, weighted streamers. Fish the lure or fly like a wounded baitfish, trolling slowly or casting and retrieving with stops and starts.

Black crappie prefer weed beds and clean water while white crappie seem to be most at home in dirty water.

Best fishing may be while the water is warming in the spring. The fish gather in large schools prior to spawning in May and June. During the spawning season, you will find crappies in bays off the main lake or river. Look for areas where the bottom is free of silt with some weed cover. After the spawn, crappies break up into smaller groups in search of food and may be found in deeper water. At this time of year, look for submerged rock piles and explore the edges of weed beds.

Crappie often inhabit the same bodies of water where smallmouth bass, largemouth bass, yellow perch and bluegill are found. But they are a strictly carnivorous fish, preferring minnows over almost everything else. For this reason, you will find crappie where they have good access to the structure minnows seek for safety. This structure may be visible to the fisherman's eye, such as a rocky cliff, a tree, a floating dock, or it might be harder to define, such as a weed bed or underwater ledge.

A boat of some type is often necessary to find the best structure areas and to follow the schools.

Outdoor writer Scott Staats and I used my canoe and Scott's knowledge of Prineville reservoir to find the fish one day in 1999. The water was low and we located an artificial shoal made from old tires. Jigging across the tires brought strikes and our first fish, but we craved more action.

We found it along a rock wall farther down the lake. Drifting downstream then paddling back up along the face of the wall, we had strikes, seemingly on every cast. The lesson was clear. Find the structure, then target crappie with techniques tailored to the fish's feed preferences and don't forget to sharpen up your filet knife. You will catch fish.

Besides being fun to catch, crappies are good on the table. Many trout fishermen are at a loss when confronted with the necessity to clean a mess of these spiny-rayed fish. The truth is that cleaning a crappie is deceptively easy.

First, start with a sharp filet knife and cut behind the gill cover down to the backbone. Second, turn the blade toward the tail and cut along the dorsal fin. Halfway along the dorsal, push the blade completely through the fish and continue to follow the backbone to the tail, cutting the filet free.

Next, lay the filet skin-side down and hold the skin against your cleaning board, sliding the knife between skin and meat, pushing toward head with a slight angle to the blade.

Now you have a boneless slice of meat, ready for batter and the frying pan.

Oregon's Brownlee and Oxbow Reservoirs, on the Snake River, offer some of the best crappie fishing in Oregon. Fern Ridge Reservoir, west of Eugene, has good numbers of crappie. Prineville Reservoir and Haystack Reservoir are the best bets for crappie in Central Oregon.

In Washington, good numbers of crappie can be found in Vancouver Lake, Columbia River sloughs, Lincoln County's Coffee Pot Lake, Washington Lake in King County, Mayfield Lake in Lewis County and hundreds of smaller lakes and ponds around the state.

Left: Buck Dietz displays a nice stringer full of crappie from a desert lake. Photo courtesy Buck Dietz and Moonlight Marine

WALLEYE

Left: Gary Lewis with a nice walleye from the Columbia River. For sheer numbers of fish, people travel to Saskatchewan. For the best chance at catching a ten-pounder or better, anglers come from all over the continent to fish the Columbia. Gary Lewis photo

The weather was unseasonably warm for April and, for the first few hours the wind was but a memory in the rimrocks. The surface of the water was smooth and glassy in the morning calm.

We were fishing the tailwater of the John Day Dam with Dick O'Brien, a longtime walleye guide on the Columbia River, hoping to pick up a few pointers and catch a few fish along the way. Kevin Shackleford of Bend, Oregon and Wade Stone of San Diego, California were my partners on this trip.

It is not known how long walleye have inhabited the waters of the Columbia River system but for the last 20 years, walleye fishing has enjoyed a tremendous upsurge in popularity in the great northwest.

Walleye have been caught in the Willamette River as far upstream as Eugene, in the lower reaches of the John Day, in the lower Washougal and in many other streams and sloughs that are connected to the Columbia.

It is not as exciting a fighter as a steelhead or a bass, but what it sometimes lacks in vigor, it makes up on the table. Walleye are among the best tasting freshwater fish. Some would argue that they are the very best tasting.

Water temperature has a lot to do with the fish's fighting ability. When the water temperature is in the low 40s the fish will tend to sulk, seeking the bottom or trying to reach some sort of structure. As the water warms, the demeanor of this big-eyed fish changes. Long runs and surface-shattering leaps are more common in the summer.

The walleye has a tapered forehead and an even body, tapering to a forked tail. It sports two dorsal fins, sharp teeth, and a big, glassy eye. Its body is green and gold, darker on the back, lighter on the belly.

For sheer numbers of fish, people travel to Saskatchewan. For the best chance at catching a ten-pounder or better, anglers come from all over the continent to fish the Columbia.

The first two weeks of April give anglers a chance at catching pre-spawn walleyes. The water is beginning to warm and the fish are healthy. Serious fishermen go in early spring for the best chance at landing a big female, full of eggs.

Walleye average four to eight pounds in the Columbia. They feed heavily on perch, northern pikeminnow (squawfish), bass, and shad. The biggest fish are females. Anglers come from all over the U.S. for a chance at catching big fish, running from ten pounds up to the current state record of 19 pounds, 15.3 ounces.

Walleye prefer deeper water than the smallmouth bass that also inhabit the Columbia and Willamette Rivers. But they are a ferocious predator and will follow their prey into very shallow water to make a kill. In general, they prefer a stone, gravel or sandy bottom. For the best walleye water look for a section of the river that has shallow spawning runs, located close to deep pools or channels.

According to O'Brien, the males move into spawning habitat first, followed by the females when water temperatures reach the upper 40's. In the Columbia, this happens in mid-April and early May.

After the spawn, walleyes again go hunting for minnows. Look for places where small fry might congregate, and do your walleye hunting there. Jetties where riprap can hold minnows, drop-offs, ledges, rocky points and gravel bars are some examples. Nightcrawlers, baby lamprey eels, and crawfish make good walleye bait.

The best walleye boat rods are seven-foot, medium-fast action models built to handle eight to twenty-pound test. Columbia River walleye are not leader shy, twelve-pound test line is a good choice. Because of the need to feed line to keep the bait down, a bait-casting reel is best for this type of work.

A walleye will often strike the bait then back off and hit it again. When using bait, it is best to, upon feeling the strike, drop the rod tip and count to three before lifting the rod tip, setting the hook. Walleye have soft mouths. The hookset should be gentle but firm and the rod should be kept arched.

O'Brien characterized the walleye bite into three classes. The first is the "suicide bite" where the fish hooks himself. The second is the "tap-tap" when the fish bites, backs off and hits again. The third is the "wet sock" where the fish closes his mouth around the bait then sulks to the bottom, angry at being fooled.

Jigs, crankbaits, spoons and spinners can also be used to good effect in walleye water. When using hardware, the walleye bite should not be "fed" as it is when bait is employed. Instead, the angler should crank a little faster to suggest the prey escaping.

Walleye are nocturnal feeders. Sunlight makes them wary. That's why the best fishing can be had

Above: Wade Stone with a big walleye from the Columbia River pool. He let this one go and kept a few smaller fish for the table. Photo by Gary Lewis

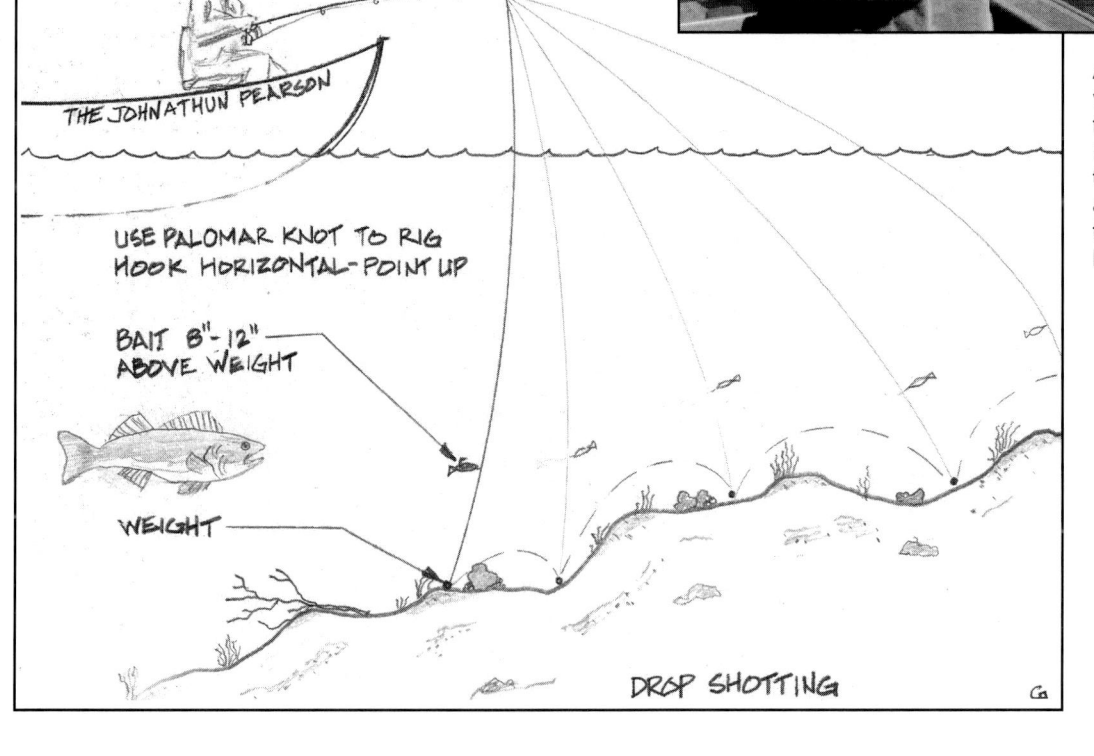

THE JOHNATHUN PEARSON

USE PALOMAR KNOT TO RIG HOOK HORIZONTAL-POINT UP

BAIT 8"-12" ABOVE WEIGHT

WEIGHT

DROP SHOTTING

at night and in the early morning hours. When the sun is at its zenith, light penetration is the best and fishing will probably be at its worst. The bite should increase from mid-afternoon to evening.

Most walleye fishermen use a boat. You can tell the novice from the expert by the way he approaches a drift. The beginner rushes up to the drift and bangs around in the boat. The old-timer slips in quiet and lets the current pull him into the drift, sometimes running the trolling motor in reverse to slow the downstream movement of the bait.

Walleye are ultra-sensitive to boat noises, silhouettes, shadows and engine noise. Whenever possible, the baits should be presented on a long line or off to the side of the boat's path of travel.

Trolling should be done at the slowest speed possible, especially in the winter time when the walleye metabolism is decreased. A 1 m.p.h. trolling speed is optimum at this time. In the summer, walleye will tolerate faster lure movement, but the troll should not exceed 5 m.p.h.

As sensitive as walleye are to boat noises and other disturbances, a wind chop on the water can make a difference in the fishing. The surface noise of the chop seems to relax the walleye, making them more vulnerable to your baits.

We fished some of O'Brien's favorite drifts, bouncing the bottom, waiting for that pull on the bait that meant a fish was working it. Close to the Oregon shore, in 27 feet of water, Kevin had a hit. He dropped his rod tip and gave line, counting to three before tightening up. The rod was bent with the weight of a good fish. He let the rod work, reeling down, then lifting - gaining line. Soon, the five-pound walleye was alongside the boat and in the net.

Our rods were rigged with three-foot leaders, light spinner blades, fluorescent green beads, and double hook rigs baited with nightcrawlers. The nightcrawler is rigged to hang straight down on the two hooks. Five inches of hollow core lead on a slider rig helped keep the bait on the bottom.

The Columbia is home for many different species. The beauty of O'Brien's walleye rig is that it is versatile. The day before our trip, one of his clients landed a thirty-pound spring chinook while fishing for walleye. Our next fish was a big northern pikeminnow that Kevin hooked in shallower water close to shore. Soon after, he caught a smallmouth bass.

We were fishing in 23 feet of water close to the Washington side when the next walleye was hooked. Wade dropped his tip, letting the fish take the bait, then he lifted and we saw the bend in his rod. The big fish was close to the bottom when she hit and, sulking, she sought to stay there while Wade applied the pressure, bringing her up.

Close to the surface, she ran again when she saw the boat, first away from it, then under. Green and gold in the water, her dorsals and fins standing erect, she pulled sideways. But she had found her match in the Californian and soon was in the net.

Heavy with eggs, the big female measured 28 inches and weighed close to ten pounds. Wade cradled it for a photo, then slipped her back into the water.

Afternoon sunlight winked on the green wavelets like a million sunlit diamonds. The east wind blew a chill down the gorge and the chop on the water promised us another fish. It struck in a shallow run close to the dam. Wade's rod bent over and we reeled in while he fought it to the boat, a two-pound male that was destined for the table.

Above: An eatin' size walleye. Photo by Gary Lewis

The best walleye fisheries in Washington and Oregon can be found in the Columbia River reservoirs from Roosevelt downstream to Bonneville Pool. Walleye have been caught as far downstream as Buoy 10 near Astoria. In Washington, Banks Lake, Potholes Reservoir, Soda Lake, Sprague Lake, and Moses Lake all contain fishable populations of walleye.

SHAD

Right: Gary Lewis with an Umpqua River shad he caught on a 3-weight fly rod. Gary Lewis photo

Below: Ron Burns with one of many shad he caught on a spring day. Photo by Gary Lewis

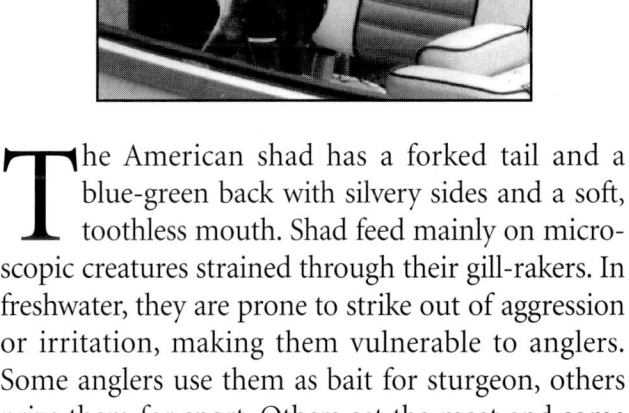

The American shad has a forked tail and a blue-green back with silvery sides and a soft, toothless mouth. Shad feed mainly on microscopic creatures strained through their gill-rakers. In freshwater, they are prone to strike out of aggression or irritation, making them vulnerable to anglers. Some anglers use them as bait for sturgeon, others prize them for sport. Others eat the meat and some eat the eggs.

Shad are the largest of the herrings that can be found on the West Coast. Imported by homesick easterners, they were introduced into Oregon and Washington in the mid-1880's. The spawning run begins when the river water warms in the spring. Mature adults average three to four pounds in size and the shad may return to the river to spawn as many as four times.

After drifting a half-mile downstream, we anchored at the head of a long pool below a riffle and a large rock, our guide Gary calls the "can-opener." We were using custom-made three-weight fly rods equipped with green twenty-pound Trilene XT Solar and twelve feet of ten-pound Maxima leader. Knotted at the end of the leader was a jig head and small pink grub. Two split shot helped keep the lure at the proper depth for the speed of the water.

I paid out thirty feet of line and began to lift the rod, then let it drop back down. The take was soft but firm. I lifted and missed, determined to set quicker next time. There! I lifted hard, and felt the fish turn, heading for the main current, using its slab-sided body to full advantage as it ripped out line.

It wasn't long before Ron had a fish on too, his four-weight fly rod bending all the way to the handle.

We caught several in the first hole then pulled anchor and drifted downstream, running several rapids. Along the way, Troy managed to boat a couple of smallmouth bass. The afternoon sun had broken through the clouds and we could see patches of blue sky now among the fleeing clouds.

There were large schools of shad in the last hole we fished. Gary anchored over a shallow shelf and we slipped our jigs in among them and hooked one after another. After awhile, Gary began to fish a little. When he brought one alongside the boat, I leaned over to net it, setting my rod beneath my knee to hold it. A shad took my bait and cut across Troy's line in its bid to get away. Downstream, Ron had another fish on.

The biggest fish of the day was one that Troy brought to the boat and Gary netted. A big female, we admired it, took a picture then sent her back into the river.

Shad are often found on shallow flats near the mouth of a tributary. Other likely spots are below rapids, falls, and dams. Such barriers stall the upstream migration and create holding areas for shad. These places afford the best fishing holes.

Light gear is preferable for shad fishing. Six-pound test line and a slow-action rod makes for a good combination for the angler who favors spinning or casting gear. Small spinners and spoons such as the Triple Teaser and others can be trolled or allowed to hang in the current. Depth is important and enough weight should be employed in fast water to take the lure close to the bottom.

The same technique is often used by those who favor jigs or shad darts. Below Bonneville Dam, a red-headed jig with a white or yellow feather body is a popular option for mining the tailrace. Other colors to try include, pink, blue, gold, and silver. Flash and color are important.

When shad can be found in slower water, a fly fisherman can find good sport. A four, five, or six-weight rod is ideal. Again, depth is key. Equipped with a sink tip line or a shooting head, the fly rodder should attempt to sink his fly into the school in the hopes of irritating an up-migrating fish.

Split shot, or colorful beads can be added to the leader to assist in keeping the fly down. Wet flies and streamers in red, white and yellow, or some combination, are the best bets.

Play the shad with firm but gentle pressure and don't rush it to the boat. A landing net is part of the required equipment when chasing shad. Their soft mouth in combination with the powerful current where most shad are caught results in many lost fish. When hooked, shad will often run straight at the boat, then veer off into the current, ripping line off the reel. Apply some pressure and they will come to the top in their attempt to throw the hook, jumping like a tarpon.

At the end of the battle, it is important to get the fish's head up on the surface. Otherwise the shad will dig in and run again, prolonging the battle. When releasing a shad, Roseburg guide Gary Lewis advocates "shocking" it back into the water instead of releasing it like a trout. Simply cradle it in both hands above the water and give it a push on its way. He believes that the released shad has a better chance of survival when handled this way.

Above: Shad darts. Photo by Gary Lewis

For sheer numbers of fish and the excitement of landing many three- to five-pounders on light tackle, shad fishing is hard to beat.

Washington anglers can find best fishing on the Columbia River at the mouth of the Washougal River and in the tailrace below Bonneville Dam. The Chehalis River, and the Willapa River also host runs of shad.

The Umpqua and Coos Rivers are good bets in southern Oregon. The largest run is found in the Columbia with shad spawning in several tributaries including the Sandy River and the Willamette. Willamette River shad can be caught near the mouth of the Clackamas and below Willamette Falls.

CATFISH

Like most other fishing pursuits, catfishing can be either as easy or as technical as you want to make it. Several species of catfish can be found in Oregon and Washington waters. Blue, black, white, flathead, channel, yellow bullhead and brown bullhead catfish all make the Pacific Northwest their home. In the mighty Columbia and in the lowliest farm pond, you can catch catfish. Brown bullheads and channel cats are most common.

Our catfish are scale-less fish with four whiskers that hang from the chin, two that hang from each side of the jaw and two barbels that grow from the snout. Catfish use their eyes, barbels and skin sensors to see, smell, taste and touch their food.

Catfish spawn when the water temperature warms in late spring and early summer, searching out spawning beds under banks, behind rocks, logs and submerged brush, and weeds. Females guard the nest while the young hatch and grow, finally leaving them on their own when they absorb their yolk sacs. Catfish are easy to catch prior to the spawn and while on the nest.

Good baits for catfish include the nightcrawler, grasshoppers, shrimp, crayfish, meat, cheese, and liver. Meat and blood baits are made commercially for cat-fishermen. Catfish will also take flies and lures

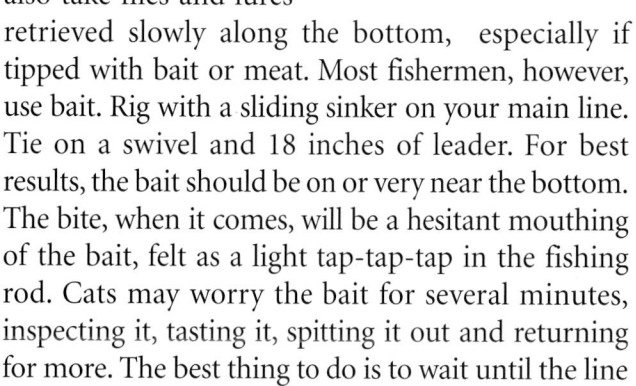

Above: Paul Pelly boated this channel cat while fishing for walleye in the Columbia. Photo by Gary Lewis

retrieved slowly along the bottom, especially if tipped with bait or meat. Most fishermen, however, use bait. Rig with a sliding sinker on your main line. Tie on a swivel and 18 inches of leader. For best results, the bait should be on or very near the bottom. The bite, when it comes, will be a hesitant mouthing of the bait, felt as a light tap-tap-tap in the fishing rod. Cats may worry the bait for several minutes, inspecting it, tasting it, spitting it out and returning for more. The best thing to do is to wait until the line begins to pull away before the hook is set.

Channel cats prefer a big, slow river or a big lake and a sandy or gravel bottom. Some of the best fishing for channel cats in Oregon is found in the mouths of the Columbia's tributaries. The John Day

River, where it empties into the Columbia is one such location. Big fish are often hooked (and sometimes landed) here, though McKay Reservoir, near Pendleton currently holds the state record for a channel cat that tipped the scale at 36 pounds, 8 ounces.

Brown bullheads are found in many farmponds around the Northwest. They are indigenous to the eastern United States but have been introduced all over the country. The brown bullhead is brown or yellowish-brown with dark barbels and a lighter-colored belly. Bullheads are often caught at night when they venture into the shallows in their hunt for food. In waters with an abundance of catfish, they can be caught all day long.

Flathead catfish prefer deep, slow pools in large rivers like the Snake and Columbia where they feed on crustaceans and fish. The current record is 42 pounds from the Snake. Like the other cats, baits are more effective than lures though the flathead will strike jigs and slow-retrieved spoons. Bounce baits on a 1/0 or 2/0 hook, close to the bottom for flatheads.

Small catfish need not be skinned before eating. Rub the slime off under running water. Some of the skin may come off with it. Frying the meat will crisp the skin and allow it to be peeled away. If the fish will be fried it is necessary to skin the fish first.

Gut and clean the fish first, then cut the head off. On a larger fish, it may be necessary to drive a nail through the fish's tail into a board. Grip the skin with pliers and peel it down.

Fillet, cut it into chunks to deep-fry, or cut into steaks for broiling or baking. Whatever your pleasure, you will come away with a new respect for the catfish.

WHITEFISH

The mountain whitefish has a forked tail, pearly-silver flanks, and an olive-brown back. Averaging fourteen inches in length, the whitefish has been known to reach five pounds. They thrive in clean water, preferring deep lakes and mountain streams.

Whitefish feed primarily on the larvae of stoneflies, caddis, and chironomids (midge flies). They also eat snails and freshwater shrimp when available. Where found in abundance, whitefish are good quarry for novice fly fishermen, because of their willingness to take small nymphs and wet flies. Bait fishermen do well with small bits of worm, salmon eggs, mealworms, crickets, and grasshoppers. When surface activity is abundant, you can catch whitefish on a dry fly. Small jigs can often produce whitefish for anglers who work shallow water in the spring. Yellow, olive, brown and black are good color choices for jig fishermen.

Small spinners tipped with bait such as white corn or a piece of worm are also good bets for whitefish.

Whitefish make good winter sport when other species are closed. Trout tackle is sufficient. A seven-foot spinning rod equipped with four or six-pound test is a good choice. For fly fishermen, four to seven weight rods are best. One good fly fishing technique to use for whitefish is to suspend a weighted nymph from a strike indicator.

Employing a casting bubble can also be a winning technique for whitefish. The casting bubble allows an angler using a spinning rod to fish flies effectively. The hollow body of the bubble can be partially filled with water to allow for long-distance casting.

Slide a casting bubble over your six-pound test main line and tie on a swivel. To the other end of the barrel swivel knot three feet of four-pound leader. In shallow rivers, you may want to use less leader. Tie on a weighted #12 brown hackle or yellow wooly worm and you're in business. Cast the rig upstream from feeding whitefish and let the current carry your fly to them, reeling slowly to keep tension on your fly. Watch the bubble. At the strike, it may stop, move upstream or drag against the current. Set the hook. After mastering the art of fishing a fly with a casting bubble, you are ready to try fishing a fly on a dropper. With two or more flies behind your bubble you stand a chance at

Above: The presence of mountain whitefish in any stream is an indicator of clean water. Whitefish are a worthy challenge and are good on the table.
Photo by Gary Lewis

catching two fish in one cast. When you find a big school of whitefish, it could happen.

In Oregon, trout anglers often catch whitefish on the Deschutes. Whitefish can be found throughout the Deschutes from its source to the mouth. The Fall River and the Crooked River can also provide good catches of whitefish. Many central Oregon lakes and reservoirs also hold large mountain whitefish.

In Washington, the Yakima River, and the Snake are good bets on the eastside and the North Fork Lewis and Skykomish host whitefish on the west side of the mountains.

Don't overlook the whitefish because of species snobbery. Some days, a whitefish will be all that you will catch on some Oregon and Washington streams. Because they are a fish that prefers cool, clean water, their very presence means that the stream you are fishing provides at least enough of that precious commodity to keep fish happy.

In some areas in Alaska, whitefish are prized for their meat. In larger supermarkets, you can find northern whitefish sold in the seafood department. Once, I had the opportunity to try some. Fried and seasoned, it was surprisingly good.

The whitefish may not have the universal appeal of the trout, but it is a worthy challenge in its own right. Some days, when the trout aren't biting, that's what you need.

NORTHERN PIKEMINNOW

I have caught northern pikeminnow on everything from dry flies to bait. Sometimes I have even caught them on purpose.

They congregate near dams, islands, jetties, river mouths, riprap, and rocky ledges. Their principal foods are salmon and steelhead smolts, crayfish, baby lamprey eels, and freshwater clams. Since salmon and steelhead smolts are disoriented after coming through dams, pikeminnow make short work of them. Northern pikeminnow have thrived in the slower water of the Columbia River since the dams were introduced. Salmon and steelhead have been the losers.

Most pikeminnow are caught downstream of dams in fast water from five to 30 feet deep. Many anglers fish at night to capitalize on the fish's tendency to move into the shallows in the dark.

Northern pikeminnow average 12 - 24 inches. Females make up the majority of the bigger fish and can reach weights of ten pounds.

Salmon and steelhead rods are good choices to use in the pursuit of pikeminnow. Ten or twelve-pound test line is adequate.

Though you can catch northern pikeminnow on a variety of gear, there are several methods that will increase your odds.

One of the most effective techniques is fishing with plastic grubs and worms from 1-1/2 inches up to 6 inches long. When fishing during the day, the best colors are smoke and chartreuse, and white. But don't be afraid to try something different. When night fishing, red, purple, and black glitter are effective. Orange-brown imitates the crayfish and can also be a good pattern.

When using grubs, a jig head is most commonly employed. The best weights are 1/8 ounce up to 1/2 ounce. When using worms, a sliding sinker is sometimes used on the leader. In faster water, the worm is left unweighted and a sliding sinker is attached to the main line.

When fishing in ten to 20 feet of water, use enough weight to "tick" the bottom from time to time. This is fishing that is hard on tackle. Expect to lose gear when fishing for pikeminnow. If you're not tying new rigs often, you're probably not fishing where the fish are.

Cast across and upstream, allowing the lure to sink and bounce. Let it drift. Strikes can be triggered, on occasion, by imparting action of some kind. Slowing down or speeding up the retrieve can pay off.

Bait fishing is another way to catch pikeminnow. Worms, liver, salmon eggs, and strips of fish are good choices. Depending on the type of fishing you do, you will need weights ranging from split shot to 1/2 ounce. Tie a No. 2 - 4 hook to an eighteen to 24-inch section of leader. Tie a swivel to the leader and slide another swivel over the main line. Use a bead to protect the knot. Tie a four-inch section of line to the sliding swivel and attach a piece of hollow-core pencil lead. A bullet sinker, or bottom-walker rig can be used in place of the sliding swivel if desired.

Spinners and spoons are also effective for pikeminnow. Again, it is important to use a lure that will sink fast enough in the swift water where these fish are found. Additional weight can be added in the form of split shot.

Trolled behind a boat, crankbaits are potent pikeminnow lures. The important thing about using crankbaits is matching the lure to the depth of the water. Use a crankbait that will dive almost to the bottom, fishing effectively in the fish-holding zone.

The Bonneville Power Administration sponsors a sport reward program designed to thin northern pikeminnow populations in the Columbia. For the first 100 fish you catch in a season, you can earn $4.00 per fish. After that, the BPA will pay up to $6.00 depending upon how many fish you turn in. Every Columbia River pikeminnow over nine inches long is worth money.

To learn more about season dates, how-to, where-to, and payment possibilities, call 1-800-858-9015 or visit the website at: www.pikeminnow.org.

CARP

In the neighborhood where I lived in my early teens, there were a lot of opportunities to catch fish if a fellow had some imagination and a bicycle he could ditch in the brush. There were trout in a few of the streams, and perch and squawfish to catch down at the river. Sometimes we fished at the yacht club until insurance regulations changed and we were kicked out. You never knew what you might hook at the yacht club. There were sturgeon, crappie, bass, and sometimes, trout. The real prize was a carp.

Somewhere I read about using doughballs for carp. So I began experimenting with dough until my mother figured out that my interest was more piscatorial than culinary. My kitchen privileges were reduced until I assured mom that I was eating my creations myself and not feeding her groceries to carp.

I never did perfect the doughball. Instead, I found that salmon eggs, left to sit on the bottom, were a worthy bait for our lower Columbia carp. If I could get the eggs to the bottom without hooking a peamouth, I had a decent chance at catching one of the big bronze minnows.

The carp's introduction to the northwest was, according to Lampman's 1946 publication, *Coming of the Pond Fishes*, due to the flooding of a Troutdale pond. In 1881, high water took the carp out to the Columbia. In less than fifteen years, they were being sold for fertilizer by commercial fishermen.

The carp is equipped with large bronze scales. They form an armor of diagonal lines creating a diamond pattern. Its mouth is supple and fleshy with twin barbels on each side of the jaw. It is classified as a rough fish and is considered by most anglers to be harmful to native species. However, it is a cautious feeder and not easily caught. Carp are not small fish. In the Columbia River system they average five to ten pounds, but have been known to reach twenty pounds and beyond. When hooked, it is a strong fighter and worthy of the respect of any angler.

Carp feed primarily on vegetation, snails, shrimp, and insect larvae. They have been known to feed on fruits and berries in season, as they tumble from streamside vines or trees and decay in the water. Opportunistic feeders, they can be caught on a variety of baits.

Serious carp anglers often concoct special baits to aid in the taking of the big minnows. Some of these baits are particle rigs, made from birdseed, nuts, corn and a binding agent to hold it all together. Boilies are another option. They are made from such things as cat food, fish pellets, liver, yeast, eggs, and other ingredients whipped into paste and boiled. If that doesn't seem to do it for

Left: Bob Pengra caught this big carp on the John Day River in eastern Oregon. It hit a spinner bait. Photo courtesy Bob Pengra

you, breads work if they are presented well and you can keep peamouth and chubs from picking at it. In what you choose to use for carp bait, you are limited only by your imagination.

One day I was fishing with some friends at the yacht club. Tired of catching smaller fish, I weighted my eight-pound test line with a slip sinker and tied on a section of six-pound test leader, to which I knotted a shiny brass No. 10 hook. On the hook, I strung two salmon eggs. Then I lowered the bait to the bottom and watched my rod.

After about 30 minutes, I saw my rod tip began to bounce. When it seemed like the fish had taken the bait, I lifted the rod and the fight was on. It thrashed and ran and pulled and bull-dogged while I kept the rod high and made sure the drag was set correctly on my big old Cardinal reel. The fight lasted about ten minutes and attracted several of the men from around the yacht club. Finally I had the fish close to the surface and could see its bronze scales reflecting the sunlight as it rolled. Steering it to the dock, I was ready to land it. My friend Joe was closest, and he reached down to grab the fish but instead grabbed the line, just as the fish made one last bid for freedom. The line snapped and the fish got away.

I guessed it was a 15-pounder, but the look in Joe's eyes made me think that it could have been bigger.

That started us fishing for carp on a regular basis. We debated the merits of nightcrawlers, balled-up Wonder Bread, salmon eggs, cheese, and corn. We found that dropping the bait to the bottom and setting the rod on the dock was the best way to entice a big one to take the hook.

There is only one problem with that theory. A carp is a big fish and he can take the rod if you don't get to it quick enough. One of my frequent fishing companions found this out one Sunday morning. He never did get his rod back.

Because of their suspicious nature and a smallish, sensitive mouth, the best carp hook is a No. 8 or 10. Single hooks work well because there is less steel for the fish to notice inside the bait, but small treble hooks work better for holding baits like dough or cheese. A sliding sinker attached to the mainline is the best way to hold the bait on the bottom in water with a current.

In calm water, consider fishing without weight so that the carp won't sense the drag on the line and spit out the bait before you can hook him.

Best carp fisheries in Oregon and Washington are in the Columbia River and in her slower-moving tributaries such as the Willamette. Sloughs and backwaters provide good opportunity as well. Lowland lakes and ponds that are subject to periodic flooding from rivers that hold carp are also good bets

---

Eight-pound test is a good choice. These fish can be big, so strong line can give you an edge. Any line over ten pound test is apt to alert the fish.

In shallow, clear water, carp can be taken on a fly rod. An eight or nine weight rod is optimum with a six-pound tippet and small larval or crustacean patterns fished close to the bottom.

Another sporting way to take carp is with bow and arrow. A reel can be attached to a bow with a line attached to an arrow. During spawning time, carp will spend more time in shallow water and can be taken by an archer who learns to compensate for refraction and motion.

Whatever method you employ to angle for carp, you will find it challenging. It is a cautious fish and hard to entice. Once hooked on light tackle, you will have a battle to remember.

In Europe and Asia, carp fishing has a devoted following. In many areas, carp is the only game around. Some of these anglers travel across the globe in search of carp.

Best carp fisheries in Oregon and Washington are in the Columbia River and in her slower-moving tributaries such as the Willamette. Sloughs and backwaters provide good opportunity as well. Lowland lakes and ponds that are subject to periodic flooding from rivers that hold carp are also good bets.

BAIT FISHING

There is art and simple pleasure in fishing with bait. I'm talking about using bait that can be found in the fish's habitat and presenting it in a natural manner. Worms, grasshoppers, crayfish, caddis larvae and eggs are my favorites. Sure, you can use snelled hooks and corn, cheese, marshmallows or gobs of fluorescent goo, but there is little skill in that.

It starts with choosing the right bait. Early in the season, the stream might be running high. Unfortunate worms are sometimes swept in when a bank crumbles into the water. Nightcrawlers or grubs are the best choice when water is running high or off-color.

String the worm on a single hook, No. 6 to 12 depending on the fish you may catch. Smaller hooks tend to be swallowed faster. If there is a possibility of hooking undersize fish, use a larger hook to make release easier.

What is the best way to put a worm on the hook?

Photo courtesy of Hot Shot Guide Service

String it on by slipping a piece of the worm along the hook shank, and letting a little dangle beyond the bend of the hook.

Any time you find grasshoppers along the bank, you can catch fish with them. My first choice is a fly rod with an imitation. But if I'm using the real thing, I like to employ a clear plastic float about three feet up from the hook to aid in casting. Float the hopper in deep water along the bank and get ready to set the hook.

Crayfish can be found in spring, summer, and fall in many waters. Tails make the best bait for most situations. String the tail on a hook, tie on a 24-inch leader and drift the bait along the bottom.

Some people call them periwinkles. They are the inch-long larvae of the Caddis fly that can be found stuck to the surface of plate-sized rocks in flowing streams. The larva makes its home in a rock case. Break open the case and pull out the yellow grub and string it on a small hook. Trout find a free-drifting caddis larva irresistible.

Single eggs are a good choice when fish are spawning. Some species lay their eggs in the spring and some in the fall. Opportunistic fish feed on the eggs that don't make it into the gravel. Fish downstream from spawning fish, drifting a single egg or two on a light leader.

It doesn't matter what type of rod you use, spin, cast or fly, but longer is better when drifting tiny baits. Nine and ten-foot rods are not too long. Extra length affords better control and allows you to slow the drift.

Your leader should be 18 to 30 inches long. For trout in the eight to fourteen-inch range, use two to four pound test. When larger fish are present, use six-pound line. Tie on a small barrel swivel to connect leader to the main line. Main line should be four to six pound test when fishing for most trout in lakes and streams.

Light line allows the best sensitivity for detecting gentle takes. Use a sliding sinker, called a bullet weight. The sinker slides along the main line and allows the fish to take the bait without feeling the resistance of split shot.

Bait fishing artists don't use bobbers. Bobbers are plastic and come in bright colors. They have little spring-loaded clips that grab the line to hold them in place.

Artists use floats made of cork or clear plastic. The float slides over the main line in place of the bullet weight. Wrap a few turns of line around a stopper or matchstick to hold the float in place.

In streams, floats are best used when a moderate current exists and snags on the bottom will take your tackle. In a lake, the float allows you to suspend the bait above the bottom or at the level of feeding trout.

When trout season opens, take a can of worms, a jar of single eggs and someone who has never fished before. Whether you are baiting a hook for the first time, or trying it again, fishing with bait can take you back to an uncomplicated age and remind you of the way it used to be.

FISHING WITH JIGS

I know it was summer because school was out and we had a couple of kids with us, but you couldn't prove it by the weather. There was snow on Paulina Peak and a stiff wind blew from the north.

We motored away from the launch and Mike turned the fish finder on as we moved into the deep water. Kokanee were the quarry and we would use jigs to bring them to the boat. I huddled into my parka and watched the fish finder. There. A ball of fish, just off the bottom. Mike continued to cruise, confident that we would find more. We did.

I stripped out line and let the jig fall, turning to look again at the screen and watching the lure dive into the school. Reeling up a few cranks, my lure was into the fish-holding zone. I lifted and dropped the tip, letting the lure flutter back down.

In the bow of the boat, Mike was doing the same thing. "Fish on," he shouted, and his rod bounced with the struggle as he sought to bring the first of many bright kokanee to the net.

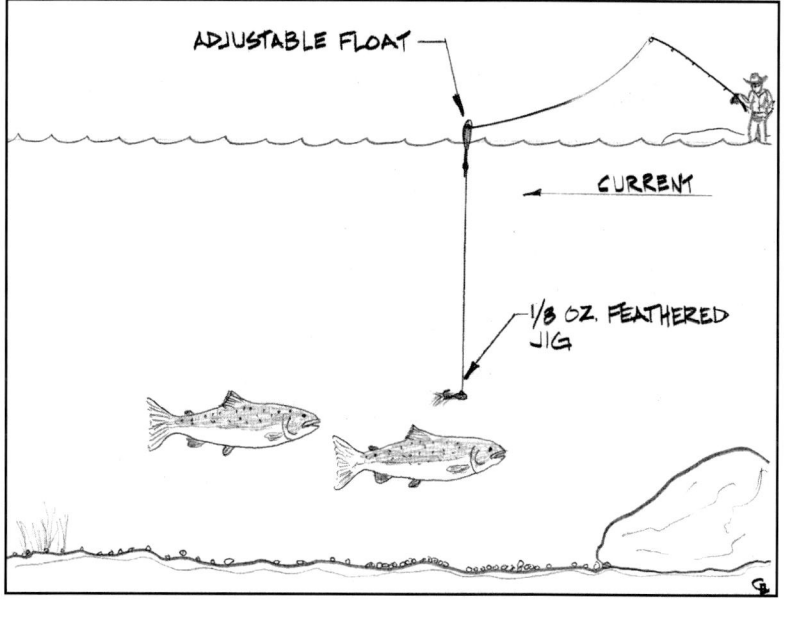

Whether the word 'jig' was first applied to a dance step or to a fishing lure, I can't say. But I do know that the jig may be the most employed, and least understood article of tackle in a fisherman's arsenal. Its very name implies motion and action, but motion is often the wrong thing to give it.

There are many types of jigs available for fishing cold water and warm water species. The simplest is a lead-head jig with a rubber skirt, most often used to catch bluegill, perch, crappie, and bass. You can impart action by moving the rod tip and catch crappie, but often, the best tactic is to fish this jig under a float, letting the gentle wave-action on the surface ruffle the jig's skirt. Another familiar version is the marabou jig, wrapped with the soft feathers that pulse in the current. Fished under a float, these jigs can be deadly for salmon and steelhead. In six feet of water, the fish will typically hold about five feet down. Rig the float to carry the lure at the fish's eye level, forcing them to make a decision when the jig drifts down on their nose. A decision to bite or retreat. Purple/pink and black/green are two of the best patterns for northwest steelhead and salmon.

Ed Iman, a top guide on the Columbia, likes to use jigs for walleyes in the spring. One of his favorite weapons is the Blue Fox Foxee, a lead-head jig with a soft, plastic body, gill-like tentacles and a

Above: Salmon/Steelhead jig with adjustable float.
Photo by Gary Lewis

Retired guide, Dana Knepper, of Central Oregon Spinnerbaits in Crescent Lake, manufactures lures for kokanee and lake trout. Knepper prefers a jig made from a brass body. He believes that the brass is key to catching more kokanee. Fishing the jig close to the bottom, the lure will tick on rocks. The ring of the brass striking stone gives a higher-pitched tone than a lead jig will produce, and this, Knepper asserts, is more attractive to kokanee.

The jig may be the most employed, and least understood article of tackle in a fisherman's arsenal

---

When fishing a jig for kokanee, the aim is to imitate a crippled baitfish. Often, the kokanee will be feeding close to the bottom. Drop the lure to the bottom, crank it up a few inches, then raise the rod tip twelve inches and let the jig flutter back down.

Anyone who has spent much time fishing for kokanee knows that lure control is very important. To achieve the optimum control, use a six to seven-foot medium action steelhead rod, and a level wind bait-casting reel.

Casting spoons and in-line spinners can also be employed as jigs for steelhead and coho. The technique is similar to that used by kokanee anglers. I've watched salmon in low water ignore a spoon only to see them strike when the same lure is jigged.

Jigs and jigging can be effective wherever there are fish to be caught. Whether you do a little dance or not is up to you.

tuft of marabou for a tail. "Tip it with a night-crawler, and fish it vertical," Iman advises. Even the slightest twitch gives motion to the jig. This is another lure where action should be limited to just the slightest of rod tip movement.

The other type of jig in common use is shaped more like a casting spoon. The Buzz Bomb is one example. Common sizes are ¾ ounce and one-ounce models. These jigs are made from lead or brass bodies and painted in different fish-catching colors. Fluorescent orange is one of the most popular finishes.

TROLLING

Trolling can be as simple as tossing a weighted, baited hook behind the boat, and pulling on the oars. It can be as complex as you want to make it, involving downriggers, charts, global positioning, and electronic fish finders. In fact, a whole book could be devoted to the subject of trolling.

There are several techniques, however, that can be employed in the pursuit of trout or salmon that will increase your odds of putting fish in the cooler. However simple or complex your equipment

Finalize your rigging when you know the water depth and visibility. You are most likely to find fish either close to the bottom or close to the surface. Identify the level where the fish are feeding, then target them there. Of all the factors that must come into play when you are trolling, depth is the key. If you're not fishing where the fish are, you're not catching.

Is the water clear or cloudy? Pick your bait and lure accordingly. Go with bigger lures and light-colored baits in dirty water and with dark colors in clear water. When using multiple spinner blades, use bigger blades when the water is murky.

Keep your hooks sharp. After every snag or fish, check the line for nicking and fraying, and touch up the point with a file. It will mean more fish in the boat at the end of the day.

Go slow when targeting most big fish. When using trolling blades, go just fast enough to keep the blades turning. The slower speed is tantalizing to fish. Go slow, but go fast from time to time. Vary the speed. Make sudden direction changes, accelerate and then slow down.

Don't troll in a straight line. Make S-turns along your course, to make your lure change directions suddenly, diving and climbing in the water column, just like a baitfish being pursued by a predator. Such direction changes trigger strikes from predatory fish.

When using a downrigger, raise and drop the rig constantly to fish more of the water column. If the bottom is relatively snag-free, drop the cannonball right on the bottom to stir up debris. Curious predators, upon investigating, will see your bait swimming out of the cloud. Hold on.

To create a scent trail when trolling soft baits, you can inject the bait with attractant or jelly. Multiple in-line spinner blades create action and vibration in the water. The flash of several revolving blades simulates a school of baitfish and draws the attention of your quarry. A similar effect can be achieved with artificial bait that leaves a trail of sparkles. The sparkles suggest tiny fish scales which trigger feeding instincts in larger fish.

Even if the fish aren't biting regularly, reel in and check your bait from time to time. The simple routine often reveals tangled leaders and weights or fouled debris on the hook. There is no worse feeling than to know the rig you have fished for the last two hours was tangled the whole time.

Develop a plan for your trolling pattern, visualize your lure working and picture what the habitat must look like down there. When you change the setup, make each component fit the purpose of the overall plan. Know your depth and keep it there.

Above: Mike Carey with a typical Paulina Lake kokanee. When trolling, sudden direction changes can spark the bite. Photo by Gary Lewis

SPINNER FISHING

TROUT

The spinner is a lure designed to attract predatory fish by flash and vibration. When retrieved, a metal blade revolves around the weighted body doing the work of attracting hungry trout. Most trout fishing in the early season takes place in lakes and ponds. Faced with hordes of anglers dangling cheese, corn, garlic marshmallows and other unfit food, hungry trout are vulnerable to a properly retrieved spinner.

When spinner fishing for trout, you need a 5 to 8-foot rod, an open-faced spinning reel, four to six-pound test monofilament line.

Anyone can catch trout with a spinner if he or she follows a few basic steps:

Pick the right spinner. 1/8 to 1/4 ounce spinners are the best choice for trout. Brass-plated, green, brown, or black painted bodies with nickel or brass blades work well for trout.

Brighter finishes work best in discolored water or in low light. Darker finishes are best in very clear water and under bright skies.

Tie the spinner directly to your main line. Avoid using snap swivels with spinners unless you are trolling.

At the lake, fish the water near rocky points, along drop-offs and near stream inlets.

When the lure hits the water, let it sink to the level of the trout and begin your retrieve, rod tip held low. Try different depths until you get a strike. To get the spinner to work its magic, it is often necessary to give it a quick tug with the rod tip. This will start the blade to turn and you will feel the pulse of the spinner in your rod.

Keep the lure moving, but not too fast. Reel too fast and trout will lose interest. Too slow and the blade will stop turning. A blade spinning constant and slow is tantalizing, almost irresistible.

STEELHEAD AND SALMON

There is no magic to enticing anadromous fish to take a spinner. Big fish like their space. Let a flashy interloper into their living room and they will react in one of three ways. One, pretend it doesn't exist. Two, run away from it. Or, three, destroy it. The only way a big fish can kill a smaller creature is to crush it in their mouth. This is the response the fisherman wants to provoke.

Left: This Deschutes River rainbow took a homemade spinner. Photo by Gary Lewis

Maximize the time that the spinner is in front of the fish. That means a tantalizingly slow retrieve. Just fast enough that the blade spins, rarely will a fish take a spinner that doesn't spin. In the case of fish holding in a riffle - cast from downstream and bring the spinner straight toward them, just above the speed of the water. They will have no choice but to hit it or get out of the way.

Like fly fishermen who tie their own flies, many spinner aficionados have turned to making their own spinners. The fisherman that makes his own lures might save a little money, but more important, he'll catch more fish by learning to tailor the spinner to water and weather.

Steelhead strike out of aggression, curiosity, defense and feeding impulses. The most common finishes on spinner blades are, in order of most flash to least flash: Silver-plate, brass, tarnished brass, nickel (mirror-finish), and black.

A basic spinner for steelhead is made from the following components: A pre-formed wire, a clevis (the C-shaped part that the blade swings on), a blade, a small bearing bead for the clevis to rotate upon, the body (usually nickel or brass), a larger bead for color or flash, a hook, and hook tubing for color.

When building spinners, tailor them to the conditions you will be facing on upcoming trips. If you will be fishing large rivers with heavy current, like the lower Deschutes, build bigger spinners. You want a lot of flash to move the fish longer distances to your lure. Build your spinners in the whole range of blade finishes with most emphasis on the flashier finishes: silver and brass.

On rivers like Washington's North Fork Lewis or Kalama, or Oregon's Umpqua and the Rogue, use medium-size spinners with brass, nickel and black finish.

Smaller rivers like the Washougal, the Salmon, the Sandy, the Santiams, the Clackamas and her tributaries, call for smaller lures. Black, nickel and tarnished brass are good producers in these rivers. Use the larger spinners in bigger pools and size down in lower, clearer water.

Almost as important as the proper size and flash of the spinner, you want to use the right color. You can add color to your spinners with plastic beads, hook tubing, and flat or prismatic tape. Fluorescent green, forest green, blue and purple are good summer to mid-fall colors for salmon and steelhead. From late fall through the cold months of winter, I like to use pinks, oranges and reds to dress up my spinners.

The decorative tape goes on the inside of the blade. Think about the spinner moving through the

Above: Dan Turner with a Klamath River rainbow.
Photo by Gary Lewis

water. The fish sees a shiny, flashing thing approaching. As it swings in front of the fish and moves on by, suddenly there is a bit of color showing. That little element of surprise is something that might spark the curiosity of the fish and incite a follow and a strike.

More important than flash or color is the presentation of the spinner, and your confidence that it will catch fish. Fish it slow so that the lure is presented in the same plane as the fish. Let it tumble, but keep the blade turning, tantalizingly slow. A fast-moving spinner is more apt to spook fish. Slow it down, almost to the point where it stops spinning.

FLYFISHING

Above: Ryan Eicher holds onto a running fish in one of his favorite runs on the upper Deschutes. Photo by Gary Lewis

It was one of those fine June evenings when the sky is blue and there is just enough breeze to keep the mosquitoes from being bothersome but not so windy that you can't cast a #12 Royal Wulff. I was watching a friend cast a fly rod for the first time.

The Deschutes was low. We hopped from boulder to boulder, fishing the pocket water. I told him that the artificial imitated a fly that had fallen to the water and was drifting downstream. "Don't let the fly drag against the current," I warned. He made large loopy casts that knotted the leader, but the trout didn't seem to mind. He caught them quickly and often, swinging them to the bank where he could release them.

We had practiced casting in the backyard. When he had a few moves mastered, we moved to the river. He had learned just enough to cast to where the fish were. The rest would have to come with practice. Fortunately, the trout were willing sparring partners.

People often debate the perfect fly fishing setup for a newcomer to the sport. The proper gear is dependent upon the water and the fish the angler will be plying.

GEAR AND TACKLE

To maximize the enjoyment, the angler should search out the best gear he or she can afford. Graphite rods are the standard of the industry, but good fiberglass rods are available, and are usually less expensive than graphite.

The rod should be between eight and nine feet long and it should be equipped with as many line guides (also called eyes) as it is long. Example given: a nine foot rod should have at least nine guides.

Fly rods are classified by line weight, length and action. The weight of rod you choose should be dependent on the type of fishing anticipated. When fishing small, slow-moving waters where the fish average eight to fourteen inches, a four or five weight rod should be adequate. If the angler alternates between fishing for small stream trout and stillwaters where the fish grow a little bigger, a five or six weight rod may be in order.

If low-water steelhead or bass are the main targets, a six-weight would be a good choice. In heavier water, where bigger fish may be encountered,

Fish on! Gary Lewis on the lower Deschutes.

a seven weight is appropriate. An eight or nine weight is preferred when salmon are the quarry.

Rods can also be classified as to action. Slow, medium and fast are the options. A fast action is a good choice for the dry fly fisherman. This is also a good choice for someone who prefers stream fishing. Stillwater anglers often prefer a medium to slow action rod when bigger fish may be encountered.

An elaborate, expensive setup is not necessary. For trout, bluegill and crappie, an inexpensive reel, loaded with 50 yards of backing and a floating line, is all that is required.

The primary function of the reel is to hold line. Most fish under fifteen inches are not played on the reel. Rather, the fisherman gains line by pulling it in with the off hand. When larger fish are more often

Left: PK Mayfly

Below: Todd Ostenson with a bright Siletz steelhead that fell for a black leech pattern. Photo by www.trophywaters.net

encountered, the fisherman should start considering higher quality reels that are balanced and equipped with a high-quality drag to slow down a running fish.

Most beginners should start with a floating line, matched to the weight of the rod. Since the fly itself is nearly weightless, the line serves as the weight needed to cast the fly.

Besides weight, fly lines are also classified as to their shape. A double taper (DT) is tapered at both ends of the line and may be the best choice in small stream presentations where casting long distances is not an issue. The weight forward (WF) line is the best choice for steelhead and salmon fishermen and anyone else who needs to cast long distances. With the weight forward line,

finesse is traded for distance. Each angler will have to make his own decision.

The leader connects the fly to the end of the fly line and is often ignored by newcomers to the sport as unimportant. It is very important to match the right leader to the fly and fish. In most cases, the leader should be tapered, starting with a heavy butt

section, graduating to lighter, more supple sections, culminating in a tippet section that is tied to the fly.

Proper coordination of leader and fly will result in well-placed casts, proper action imparted to the fly and, hopefully, more fish brought to hand.

Commercial knotless tapered leaders come in 7-1/2 feet, 9 feet and 12 feet. The beginner should match the leader to the length of the rod, but eventually, the size you want to use will be dictated on fish and conditions.

CASTING

Casting lessons can start inside with a fly rod tip section and a length of thick yarn. The rod is brought from one o'clock to eleven o'clock. The yarn's weight and bulk simulate fly line action. Before starting the back cast, wait until the line straightens out. Come back to one o'clock. WAIT until the line straightens out behind you before beginning the forward cast.

This, to me, is the essence that the flyfisherman seeks to capture. The sight, the stalk, and a skillful presentation, resulting in a sip and a splash

Once the yarn presentation is mastered, the novice fly angler has the basics of fly-casting licked. It is time to graduate to a real rod in the backyard loaded with a reel, backing, line, leader and hookless yarn "fly".

Mark out a spot in the yard and practice casting the fly to it. At the end of the back cast "pull", let your

Above: Paul Hansen displays a green drake that just crawled away from its shuck. Photo by Gary Lewis.

wrist "break" at the one o'clock mark, allowing the rod to incline toward vertical. STOP at the end of each "pull" and "push" stroke, forcing the rod to work.

This is called false casting. On the stream, it is used to air-dry the fly and feed line into the cast.

With your off hand, pull line from the reel, feeding it into the loop you are casting.

Watch other fly fishermen. What are they doing wrong? What are they doing right? Concentrate on improving your form and precision. Longer casting will follow form.

Left: Keith Ridler casts for trout on the Deschutes River. Photo by Gary Lewis

Once you have mastered the act of casting, you are ready to fish. You can learn more about casting by finding yourself a teacher. Most fly shops are eager to help a newcomer to the sport. Other techniques you will want to master include the Roll Cast, the Steeple Cast and the Stutter Cast.

SOME STRATEGIES

The best teacher is the stream itself, preferably a small stream with pocket water and eager trout. In a typical freestone creek or small river, the water creates a cyclic pattern of riffles, runs and pools.

Fishing to visible trout is one of the best ways to increase your enjoyment of the sport. Stalking is an apt name because the fisherman becomes a predator, hunting for feeding fish

---

The riffle is the fastest moving portion of any section of stream. It may average from six inches to six feet deep depending on water flow and size of the stream. It has a bottom of gravel, boulder or smooth stones.

Downstream from the riffle, the action of the water has carved out a run. The water slows and the stream widens.

The run becomes a pool. On a slow-moving stream, the pool will be far wider than the riffles and run.

Where do you fish? Spend some time watching the stream. Note the smooth spots in the run that indicate a submerged boulder. Look for underwater features that divert current and disrupt flow. Look for external components, such as overhanging banks, fallen trees and bridges that provide shade and protection for fish.

When fishing for stream trout, remember that the stream brings food to the fish. Think about

Above: A big fish took my tippet, time to tie on another length of line. Photo by Gary Lewis

where a fish is most likely to feed. Where can the fish rest, yet watch the current that brings him his dinner?

The riffle concentrates the food, but also concentrates the current, making it costly in terms of energy to feed for long in a riffle. The biggest trout will often be found where the concentration of food coincides with the end of the riffle and the beginning of a slower current.

Watch the stream and look for feeding fish. Dry flies are most often fished to imitate the downstream drift of a fallen or hatching insect. Seek to match the size, shape and color of the natural insects you find streamside. If there are no insects to be found, fish an attractor fly like the Royal Coachman or Renegade. Fish the dry fly "dead" without imparting any action or retrieve to the imitation. Cast from concealment and place the fly upstream from the feeding fish and let it drift over his lair.

Much of what a trout eats is underwater. Nymphs, wet flies, and streamers are the flies used underwater. The nymph imitates the young of an insect that hasn't completed its metamorphosis. It can be fished on a dead drift or a slow retrieve. The important thing is to keep your line tight or to watch a strike indicator that you have fastened to the butt section of your leader.

Essential NW Patterns

Above: Paul Hansen nets a Deschutes River rainbow for Gary Lewis. Gary Lewis photo

Trout Flies

Adams
Elk Hair Caddis
Joe's Hopper
Brown Hackle
Wooly Bugger
Muddler Minnow
Zonker
Hare's Ear
Prince Nymph
Copper John

Steelhead Flies

Articulated Leech
Skunk
Egg Fly
Teeny Nymph
Purple Peril
Babine Special
Freight Train
Mack's Canyon
Egg-Sucking Leech

Bass and Panfish Flies

Mouserat
Beetle
Bunny Leech
Panfish Popper
Zonker

Trout take most nymphs with little energy expended. Don't expect slashing strikes. Often, a feeding trout will simply open his mouth to inhale a nymph. If the nymph happens to be your fly, you may see an almost imperceptible movement of the line. Set the hook.

Wet flies imitate the stage between nymph and emerging dry fly. These are flies that have a swept-back collar of hackle indicating the shedding of the nymphal shuck and the presence of wings. This is a type of fly that can be retrieved in a swimming manner, or let to dead drift on a tight line.

When fishing wet flies and nymphs, it is important to let the fly sink to the desired depth. When casting into current, it may be necessary to cast farther upstream to give your fly enough time for it to sink.

Streamers imitate minnows, sculpin, eels, and crayfish, all trout favorites. Fish the streamer with a drift and retrieve consistent with the behavior of the natural. Minnows travel with darting movements, staying close to cover. Sculpin stay close to the bottom. Crayfish stay even closer to the bottom and travel backwards in great thrusts of their tail.

The Muddler Minnow is one of the all-time great fly patterns of our era. It resembles a small sculpin and can be deadly on stream trout when fished on a floating or sink tip line. Cast up and across, letting the current swing your fly on the leader. The fly will resemble a bottom-dwelling sculpin that is too far from home.

The current drags the fly up to the top while your fly line pulls it down. Retrieve the Muddler in three to four-inch strips that indicate the panic escape of the sculpin.

When fishing smaller streams and rivers, how you approach makes the difference between having a good day on the water and catching bigger fish. The idea is to spot the fish before the fish spots you.

You can get the best practice without a fly rod in your hand. Just go to observe. You may learn a lot more if you are not trying to catch one.

Look for parts of the fish. A tail or a fin may catch your eye first. The trout might just look like a gray shadow against the gravel, or a hint of olive against an underwater boulder. Sometimes you can see one roll on its side, nose in the gravel. When you see a flash of silver, keep looking, you may see it again. Then go back to your car, get your rod, and tie up with a weighted nymph.

In stillwater, where I can look into the shallows, I watch for trout feeding in the weeds at the water's edge. Often, all I see is a nose or a tail. Sometimes the fish are close enough to touch.

Remember that if you can see the fish, the fish can see you. Stay out of sight if you want to catch him. When stream fishing, the fish is facing upstream. You want to make your cast from downstream, behind him. Keep something between you and the fish: a bush, a tree or a boulder. Stay low. The closer you get to the fish, the lower you must be.

Walk soft, approach from downstream, and use the concealment nature has provided.

Fishing to visible trout is one of the best ways to increase your enjoyment of the sport. Stalking is an apt name because the fisherman becomes a predator, hunting for feeding fish.

This, to me, is the essence that the flyfisherman seeks to capture. The sight, the stalk, and a skillful presentation, resulting in a sip and a splash.

When you slow down to observe the water before you cast, when you take the time to observe fish feeding patterns, you will catch fish that other people miss.

FLY TYING

There is one fly that is responsible for catching more fish than any other in our time. Beginners and experts alike use the Wooly Bugger to advantage. Tied in various colors, and sizes, it can imitate a host of aquatic creatures upon which trout, salmon, bass and panfish feed. Best of all, it is one of the easiest flies to learn to tie

Assemble the following tools and materials:

Vise, bobbin, bodkin

Hook: Mustad 9672 or equivalent hook. No. 6 or 8

Thread: Black or color to match body

Tail: Black, purple, brown, olive, or red marabou

Body: Small or medium diameter black, purple, brown, olive chenille.

Hackle: Black, grizzly, or color to match body

Step 1:

Secure the bend of the hook in vise as shown in photo with hook shank horizontal. Start the thread on the hook shank by turning a few wraps of the running end over the tag. When thread is secure, clip off the tag.

Step 2:

Expose the soft marabou of a hackle feather and strip a few fibers away. Lay the fibers along the hook shank as shown and tie down with several firm turns of the thread.

Photos by Tiffany Lewis

Step 3:

Trim marabou from a hackle feather and tie in at base of tail with several wraps of thread. Wrap thread to the eye.

Step 4:

Cut a three-inch length of chenille and tie off at tail. Wrap chenille along shank of hook to just before the eye and secure it with the thread. Trim off tag end of chenille.

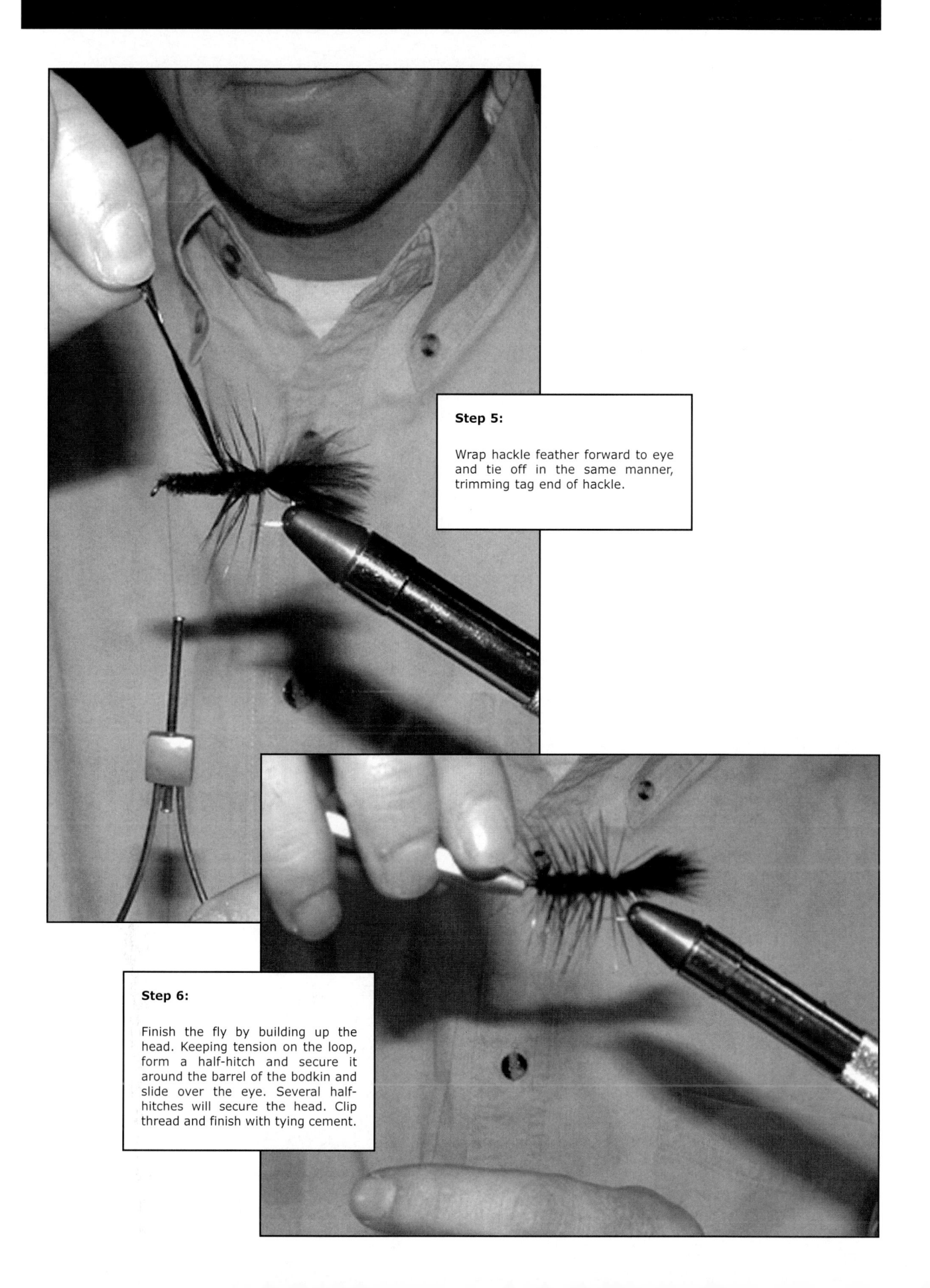

Step 5:

Wrap hackle feather forward to eye and tie off in the same manner, trimming tag end of hackle.

Step 6:

Finish the fly by building up the head. Keeping tension on the loop, form a half-hitch and secure it around the barrel of the bodkin and slide over the eye. Several half-hitches will secure the head. Clip thread and finish with tying cement.

READING WATER

Above: The current brings much of what a trout eats to him. All that most fish below a certain size need to do is to wait. Dinner will come. Photo by Roger Carbone

Reading a stream means more than looking at currents on the surface

There are two ways to approach fishing a stream. The first is to look for visible fish and then to make the presentation. The second is fishing on faith. This refers to anytime when there are no fish to be seen but you know that they must be there. To successfully fish blind requires that you can guess the spots in the river where the fish are most likely to be found.

A trout needs three basic things: oxygen, shelter and food.

Oxygen. In general, oxygen in cold water is not a problem. What happens in the warmer months is that the trout's metabolism has increased and he needs more oxygen from the water around him. As the temperature of the water increases, the amount of oxygen that it can hold decreases. When the stream thermometer

Above: Careless caddis and unfortunate ants are caught in the current and drift to waiting trout. Watch foam and bubble lines for the clues to where to find feeding fish. Photo courtesy www.numbbutt.com

registers above 70 degrees, the trout are in danger of suffocating. Unless they can get to whitewater. The more turbulent the water, the more air is getting into it.

Shelter. Everything that will eat a fish (except another fish) comes from above. When a trout is a fingerling, a kingfisher might get him. A little older, a little bigger and blue herons will be stabbing their beaks at him. When he makes it to pan-frying size, then fishermen are interested in turning him into crispy brown fillets. So trout go where you and the birds can't see them. They'll hide just off the bottom of deep holes, under cut banks, sulk in the lee of a boulder or under a fallen log where a bird cannot swoop down and take them. Unless they've been spooked, they will be within easy striking distance of dinner.

Food. The current brings much of what a trout eats to him. All that most fish below a certain size need to do is to wait. Dinner will come. But there are certain spots in a stream where the food is concentrated. Imagine yourself sitting at a table in a busy restaurant. There is food all around you. Are you hungry? You might just go cruising from table to table picking off the choicest morsels. But that's a lot of work. Where is all the food coming from? You look around. Waiters are bringing it from the kitchen. Wouldn't it be smartest, as long as you are going to take it anyway, to intercept them as they come out? Sure, a few bites will get by you as you are eating the lobster but the small-fry need to eat too. If only so you can eat them later.

This is how a big trout thinks.

And so this is how you should think in order to hook him. Often there is a foam or bubble line that drifts with the current. This is where the careless caddis, the unfortunate ants and grasshoppers are swept and where the larger trout line up to eat. Before you make your first cast, determine which is the best spot for a trout to wait. On a smaller stream, you can often catch the best fish first by making a good cast to the best feeding lie.

But this is the easy stuff, seeing what is happening on the surface. To really read a trout stream requires that you take all the parts that make up a particular stretch of water and see how they fit together.

Imagine this spot on central Oregon's Metolius River. Upstream, the water froths over smooth fist-sized stones, to break into a deeper pool. On the far side, the water is shallow, a shelf of rock, just five inches of water covering it. In the middle is a deep channel sloping up on the near side. The water sweeps around in a back-eddy piling up debris over the seasons in a dark blend of bark, leaves, twigs and pine needles. Downstream, on the near side, is a log, underwater and half-buried by silt. There is a deep cut under the log facing out into the channel. At the end of the pool, the water is hastened on its way as the water shallows and the banks constrict.

To really read a trout stream requires that you take all the parts that make up a particular stretch of water and see how they fit together

---

You can't see the bottom here, but you can see a bulge on the surface of the water, just ahead of the tailout. There is something there. Probably a rock and that rock is protection. Protection from danger, shelter from the current, but close enough to the food-carrying current where a fish could rise up, grab a bite and ease back down. A fish could lie behind the boulder or in the dead spot in front of it. If the boulder is large enough, there could be several fish in its shelter.

There are probably trout holding on the outside edge of the submerged log as well. Upstream, the eddy swirls around giving fish more time to look at their food. Imagine going below the surface and watching the bubble line from below. Where would you go to stay out of the heavy current yet still be close enough to take the food you wanted? Where would you go when predators with sharp beaks or nine-foot flyrods came too close?

Bring polarized glasses and don't string your flyrod until you've watched the water for some time. Now you're reading a trout stream. The story it tells you and the story you can tell later depend on what you do next.

PHOTOGRAPHY

Memories are the greatest by-product of our fishing and hunting adventures. They last a lot longer than bread-battered trout. The perfect way to preserve them is through photographs.

With the advent of high-tech, low-budget 35mm point-and-shoot cameras, taking great pictures is now easier than ever.

Let's start with film speed. Use 100 ASA for bright, clear days and when the utmost clarity is desired. Use 200 ASA for the times when light levels will be less certain and when morning or evening shots are more likely. Use 400 ASA for darker days, dense cover and action shots.

If you are using a digital camera, forget the part about film speed. Your camera does that part for you. But the other rules of photography still apply.

Lighting is important to your final product. Eric J. Hansen is a professional outdoor photographer living in Corvallis, Oregon. He pays close attention to lighting and refuses to waste film during poor lighting conditions. Want to take better pictures outside? Remember his simple photographic rule: You can take a bad picture in good light but you can't take a good picture in bad light

Anyone who carries a camera outdoors knows that sometimes the best scenery looks flat when the photo is developed. The difference between good outdoor photography and bad is often at the whim of old sol. So how do you tell when the sunlight is optimum for taking pictures?

Simply stand a pen or pencil on one end and look at its shadow. If the shadow is shorter than the object casting it, leave the camera in the bag. If the shadow is longer than the pencil, your chances of taking fabulous photos are fantastic.

Take a little time to arrange your subject. If you keep a brook trout to eat, wipe the blood and pine needles off and take the picture before it starts losing its brilliant color. Taking care of these details will pay off in better pictures.

Pay attention to framing your subjects. What do you want to include in the photo? Mountains, the river, a canyon, a waterfall, or an old cabin? Including landscape in a photo of an angler and his catch can be accomplished by positioning the subject at one side of the picture with the landscape stretching out to the other.

Pose a subject so light shines on the face, without forcing them to look into direct sunlight. And the subject should take off the fishing glasses. Eyes are what connect viewer to subject. With eyes concealed the subject is remote and less interesting. Watch for shadows thrown by hat brims. When all that is peeking out from under a hat is a nose, it turns a good picture comical. Tip the hat back and use flash to fight shadows.

Most of these pictures are taken with the photographer and the subject both standing. For variety, take some pictures from below to add an element of immediacy. Have the subject extend the fish toward you to emphasize it and hold viewer interest.

Another standard photographic rule is the rule of thirds. Put your subject in one third of the frame, on either side of the middle to draw the viewer's eye into the scene. If the horizon is visible in the frame, position it so that it is in either the bottom third or the top third of the photo. Don't split the frame with the horizon.

There is more to fishing than just the catching, so snap more than the catches. Photograph the action, the stalk, the hookset, the fight, netting the fish, letting it go. Take pictures of the wildlife you see, of a waterfall or a rock formation. But remember that the most interesting pictures have people in them. So snap your buddy taking a nap along the trail or looking downstream, his rod resting on his shoulder. Snap your companions at the car, pausing for lunch or laughing over a campfire.

Another option is black and white. It costs a little bit more to have developed but since most prints are made in color, black and white lends drama to a photo album. If you are shooting digital images, your software has the ability to change the images you shot in color to black and white or sepia tones. Experiment with your photos to create different effects.

Experiment with different compositions. Keeping a few trout? Take pictures of the day's catch laying next to a flyrod and an open flybox. Be right there when your buddy reaches for the bass he's just subdued. Catch the light in a little girl's eyes when she tentatively touches her first bluegill. The combinations are endless.

CATCH & RELEASE

This is the dirty little secret about improper catch and release. The angler smiles, and gets a firm grip on the fish while the picture is taken. A warm glow of satisfaction and of doing something worthwhile fills him as he watches the trout kick away. Too often, the trout dies.

Catch and release fishing is not nobler than keeping a fish for dinner. It is, though, often the right thing to do if you want to enjoy good fishing in the future.

Anyone who decides to turn a fish loose has an obligation to return it to the water, giving it as good a chance to survive as possible. From the moment you hook a fish to the instant when it kicks away from your cradled hands, your highest duty is to preserve its life. If not, then preaching the mantra of catch and release is idle talk.

A small percentage of released fish die, no matter how much care is taken during the fight and subsequent handling. Often, it is their own will to throw the hook that kills them. Sometimes, it is the way they are hooked that seals their fate.

Being sensitive to the fragility of life, the careful angler can reduce to a tiny fraction, the number of fish that die after being hooked and released. It starts with the method of take. Fish that are caught on bait are most vulnerable. Often the hook is taken deeper in the mouth, or almost in the stomach if the fish is allowed to swallow the bait before the hook is set.

When treble hooks are used, the potential for damage is increased, as more hooks can create more wounds. If the fish is bleeding, the chances that it will die are increased. Pinching the barbs down ensures that a smaller wound will be created.

At the end of the battle, the fish should not be removed from the water if the intent is to let it go. Avoid using a net, if you can. If you must use a net, use one made of rubber which won't remove the fish's essential protective slime. Don't touch the eyes or the gills. Reach down and slip the hook out. If the fish has taken the hook deep, cut the line and trust the fish's stomach acids to destroy the hook in a few days. The fish still has a good chance of survival if you handle it with care.

If a picture is desired, have the cameraman ready to snap the instant it is lifted from the water.

Next, point the fish upstream and cradle it in both hands, underwater. Gently rock it back and forth to prompt the opening and closing of the gills in the normal breathing pattern. Be patient, wait until the fish begins to move on its own again. If the fish begins to lean one way or the other, keep rocking it until, rested, it kicks away.

Give it as much time as it takes to swim away under its own power. The future of your fishing might depend on your patience.

Left: Gentle handling will ensure this fish will survive. Photo by Gary Lewis

RECIPES

Shoreside Salmon Barbecue

A fish as worthy as a Pacific Northwest salmon or steelhead should be served in style. Here's one way to do it right, courtesy Greg Price of Deschutes River Outfitters. - Gary Lewis

Salmon or Steelhead Fillets

Butter

Lemon (sliced)

Lime (sliced)

Red Onion

Dill

Salt

Pepper

Cayenne pepper (optional)

Prepare a bed of foil with the edges folded up to contain the sauce. Lay fillets skin side down on the foil. Salt and pepper thoroughly. Place slices of butter on the meat. Alternate slices of lemon and lime on meat. Slice red onion and apply onion liberally. Coat with dill. Salt and pepper again. For an extra kick, add cayenne pepper. Cook on the barbecue until the meat is flaky. Remove skin and fat with a filet knife, then serve with garnishes on top.

Baked Salmon Fillets

Gary Lewis Recipe

2 pounds Salmon or Steelhead Fillets

2 tablespoons Lemon Juice

Butter

1 teaspoon Johnny's Seafood Seasoning

Lemon (sliced)

¾ cup Mayonnaise

2 teaspoons Dried Dill Weed

Oil the baking dish. Lay fillets in the dish. Lightly butter fillet then sprinkle with lemon juice and seafood seasoning. Spread mayonnaise and then sprinkle with dill weed. Leave uncovered. Bake at 375 degrees for about 30 minutes or until meat is flaky. Garnish with sliced lemons and parsley.

Flaky Broiled Walleye Fillet

Maybe the best-tasting fish to be found in the Pacific Northwest's freshwaters, walleye can be fixed many different ways. This recipe is courtesy of my walleye angling mentor Dick O'Brien. We'll miss you Dick. - Gary Lewis

Walleye fillets

Mayonnaise

Lowry's Seasoning Salt

Prepare a bed of tinfoil and fold up the edges to hold in the juices. Slather the fillets with a liberal dose of mayonnaise. Shake on a coat of Lowry's Seasoning Salt. Broil until meat is flaky, then serve.

Broiled Shad Roe Appetizer

Gary Lewis Recipe

Broiled shad roe isn't for everybody, but if you simply must eat fish eggs, this is the best way to do it. - Gary Lewis

4 Shad roe

4 Slices of bacon

2 Tbsp melted butter

2 Lemons

Set oven on broil to preheat. Wash and soak roe in salt water for ten minutes. Remove from salt water and rinse. Wrap the roe in bacon. Broil for five minutes. Turn over and broil for seven minutes or until bacon is done. Cut each skein in half and garnish with bacon and lemon wedges. Pour melted butter over roe and serve.

TAXIDERMY

Early on opening morning, as the fog was still coming off the water, you wrapped your hands around the cup of coffee and watched the tips of the rods and saw the gentle action of the plug working. The hum of the trolling motor and the lapping of wavelets against the bow were the only sounds that mattered.

It was the first fish of the day and the biggest and it bent your rod nearly double in the rod holder, as line peeled off your reel and you spilt your coffee on the floor of the boat.

Some fishing memories can be preserved through taxidermy. In years to come, looking at that trophy rainbow mounted over the fireplace will take you back in time to that moment when you first saw it, framed in droplets of water above the surface, its back arched against the sky.

A good taxidermist can make him seem to come alive again. When you catch a memory to preserve in taxidermy you have two options: a skin mount, or a fiberglass reproduction.

A skin mount is made from the skin of your fish mounted on a foam mannequin and painted to recreate the brilliant color your fish had the moment you slid the net under it.

The decision to have a fish mounted should be made while the fish is still in the net. Everything you do after taking it from the net can have either a positive or negative effect on the quality of the finished product. Do not gut the fish or put it on a stringer. Instead, wrap it in a wet towel and lay it flat in an ice chest. Picture how you want the fish to appear. Will you want its left side to face the living room? Then lay it on its right side in the cooler. Freeze the fish or bring it immediately to the taxidermist.

The taxidermist traces and measures your catch to find an appropriate form or help him carve a custom fish body from a block of foam.

Tails, fins, barbels, and head features are subject to shrinkage, so many taxidermists take molds and reproduce these parts in fiberglass. This replicates the fine details that make each fish different.

Next, the skin is separated from the carcass and all meat and fat is removed. The skin is then tanned to preserve the natural markings. Degreasers are used to promote longevity.

After tanning, the skin is placed on the mold. The artist fits all the parts back together, then blends the unions with sculpting compound. The

photos you took when the fish was caught will come in handy when the taxidermist is ready to paint. Otherwise, he will use reference photos to match your fish's color to the time of year your trophy was landed.

The decision to have a fish mounted should be made while the fish is still in the net

---

Every step your taxidermist takes is important in the process. Any shortcuts will cheapen the final product. When shopping for a taxidermist, look closely at his representative work, examining every detail.

Fiberglass reproductions are made to replicate the fish you released (or ate). One of the biggest things you can do for your taxidermist is to take pictures of your trout right after it is subdued, so that the artist will be able to match the fish's original coloring. Take measurements of the fish with a cloth tape. Measure from tip of nose to tip of tail, then measure the girth, just in front of dorsal fin.

The main advantage of using a fiberglass reproduction is that you can eat the fish or let it go after taking photos and a few measurements. Your trophy will be an exact replica of the fish that you let go, created from fiberglass and gel coat, hand-painted and detailed.

Most taxidermists provide some type of display with their work. Think about how you want to display your trophy, then have the conversation with your taxidermist before you make your deposit.

BOATS

Boating is a way of life for many Northwesterners. From the float tube to the party boat, from the canoe to the pleasure yacht, they can all be used for fishing. Selecting the right boat is not easy, but it is an important part of getting maximum enjoyment from freshwater fishing.

Selecting a Boat

More than 2,000 boat manufacturers build boats in the United States. Most manufacturers have multiple models for you to choose from. So what boat is best for you? Most boats are built with a specific purpose. Consider how you will use the boat most of the time. Will it be a boat for drifting quiet rivers, whitewater, shallow water lakes, deep water lakes, or backwater ponds?

Hull design is a very important part of the equation. Flat bottom boats are good for shallow water and plane easily when the boat is under power, but flat bottom boats are uncomfortable when running the waves. Drift boats, jet sleds, jon boats and utility boats all are built with flat bottom hulls.

Vee hull and deep vee hull boats run smoother in rough water than flat bottom boats, but require more power to move through the water than other hull types. Jet sleds for bigger rivers are often built with deep vee hulls. Round bottom boats, such as canoes, cut through the water easily but have more tendency to roll.

Party boats, sailboats, pontoon boats and catamarans use multi-hull construction for greatest stability.

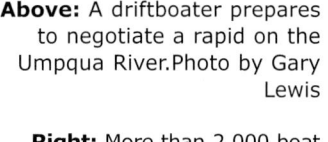

Above: A driftboater prepares to negotiate a rapid on the Umpqua River. Photo by Gary Lewis

Right: More than 2,000 boat manufacturers build boats in the United States. Most manufacturers have multiple models for you to choose from. So what boat is best for you?

Top Right: Photo by Kevin Jurgens, The Garage

Do you fish alone? A float tube or pontoon boat might be the answer. If your tastes run to stillwaters and slow-running rivers, a canoe might be your best bet. Will fishing be the primary activity or will you use the boat for other activities such as hunting or camping? If so, an aluminum fishing boat might a better choice.

If you love rivers and whitewater, a drift boat or a jet sled might be the best choice. Know the regulations on the rivers in your area before you buy. If a jet sled makes the most sense for you, you have another decision: flat bottom or vee hull. On bigger rivers like the Deschutes, Snake and Columbia, the vee hull will give you a better ride when traveling long distances. On rivers like the Lewis and Cowlitz, where you may have to run in four inches of water, over gravel bars, a flat bottom boat is the way to go.

Every boat, regardless of size should carry a life preserver or buoyant cushion for each person aboard. Every motorboat should have one or more fire extinguishers aboard. An anchor should be aboard. Carry several lines of different lengths for use when tying up to a beach or tying off to a timber or dock.

Consider carrying a compass in your boat if you will be navigating some of the region's larger lakes. Thick fog can disorient a boater on anything bigger than a farm pond. Depending on the size of your boat and the length of your trips, other equipment should include a flashlight, flares, a first aid kit, a whistle or fog horn, an extra paddle or oar and a tool kit.

Boaters need different fishing tackle than bank anglers. A bank angler can get along without owning a net. You need a net if you will be fishing from a boat. Make sure it has a long handle so you don't have to lean over the water to bring in a big fish. Long rods are a liability on a boat. When sturgeon fishing on the bank, a ten-foot rod makes sense. When fishing from a boat, use something in the six- to seven-foot range. Rod holders make life easier on a boat. Consider having rod holders to use while fishing and rod racks for safe storage while not in use.

How to Weigh a Fish for the Record Book

If you think the fish you just landed is a candidate for the record books, you need to act fast.

Follow these steps:

❶ Keep the fish in water or on ice while in transit to a certified scale.

❷ Weigh the fish on a certified scale (grocery store) as soon as possible.

❸ Obtain signatures and contact information of scale operators and witnesses.

❹ Take side-view photos of fish.

❺ Take the fish to a Department of Fish and Wildlife office for verification.

❻ Fill out a state record application and have witnesses endorse it.

For information on boating rules and regulations, contact the Oregon State Marine Board at: www.marinebd.osmb.state.or.us or call (503) 378-8587

RECORDS

COLD WATER RECORDS Oregon Game Fish Records - Updated March 10, 2003

Species	Weight	Year	Where	Angler
Brook Trout	9 lbs 6 oz	1980	Deschutes River	Burt Westbrook
Brown Trout	28 lbs 5 oz	2002	Paulina Lake	Ronald Lane
Bull Trout	23 lbs 2 oz	1989	Lake Billy Chinook	Don Yow
Coastal Cutthroat	6 lbs 4 oz	1984	Siltcoos Lake	Kay Schmidt
Lahontan Cutthroat	9 lbs 8 oz	1986	Malheur River	Phillip Grove
Golden Trout	7 lbs 10 oz	1987	Eagle Cap Wilderness	Douglas White
Lake Trout	40 lbs 8 oz	1984	Odell Lake	H.V. Hannon
Rainbow Trout	28 lbs	1982	Rogue River	Mike McGonagle
Steelhead	35 lbs 8 oz	1970	Columbia River	Berdell Todd
Chinook Salmon	83 lbs	1910	Umpqua River	Ernie St. Claire
Chum Salmon	23 lbs	1990	Kilchis River	Roger Nelson
Coho Salmon	25 lbs 5.25 oz	1966	Siltcoos Lake	Ed Martin
Atlantic Salmon	No record as of March 10, 2003			
Kokanee Salmon	6.74 lbs	2001	Wallowa Lake	Pam Fahey
Striped Bass	64 lbs 8 oz	1973	Umpqua River	Beryl Bliss
Shad	5 lbs 13 oz	1994	Columbia River	Patricia Ann Young
Whitefish	4 lbs	1974	McKenzie River	Todd Fisher

WARM WATER RECORDS Oregon Game Fish Records - Updated March 10, 2003

Species	Weight	Year	Where	Angler
Hybrid Bass	18 lbs 8.32 oz	2002	Ana Reservoir	Justin Marks
Largemouth Bass	12 lbs 1.6 oz	2002	Ballenger Pond	Adam Hastings
Smallmouth Bass	7 lbs 14 oz	2000	Henry Hagg Lake	Kevin Silver
Striped Bass	64 lbs 8 oz	1973	Umpqua River	Beryl Bliss
Bluegill	2 lbs 5.5 oz	1981	Farm Pond	Wayne Elmore
Bullhead Catfish	3 lbs 7 oz	2001	Henry Hagg Lake	Bob Judkins
Channel Catfish	36 lbs 8 oz	1980	McKay Reservoir	Boone Haddock
Flathead Catfish	42 lbs	1994	Snake River	Joshua Kralicek
White Catfish	15 lbs	1989	Tualatin River	Wayne Welch
Black Crappie	4 lbs 6.1 oz	1995	Corvallis Pond	John Doss
White Crappie	4 lbs 12 oz	1967	Gerber Reservoir	Jim Duckett
Yellow Perch	2 lbs 2 oz	1971	Brownsmead	Ernie Affolter III
Sacramento Perch	11.2 oz	1998	Lost River	Jonathan Cogley
Green Sunfish	11 oz	1991	Umpqua River	John Baker
Pumpkinseed Sunfish	7.68 oz	1996	Lake Oswego	Linda Mar
Redear Sunfish	1 lbs 15.5 oz	1992	Reynolds Pond	Terence Bice
Walleye	19 lbs 15.3 oz	1990	Columbia River	Arnold Berg
Warmouth	1 lbs 14.2 oz	1975	Columbia Slough	Jess Newell

COLD WATER RECORDS Washington Game Fish Records - Updated April 30, 2002

Species	Weight	Year	Where	Angler
Atlantic Salmon	8.96 lbs	1992	Goat Lake	Gregory Karl Lepping
Sea-run Atl Salmon	14.38 lbs	1999	Green River	Ron Howard
Brook Trout	9 lbs	1988	Wobbly Lake	George G. Weekes
Brown Trout	22 lbs	1965	Sullivan Lake	R.L. Henry
Bull Trout	22 lbs 8 oz	1961	Tieton River	Louis Schott
Cutthroat Trout	12 lbs	1961	Lake Crescent	W. Welsh
Sea-run Cutthroat	6 lbs	1943	Carr Inlet	Bud Johnson
Lahontan Cutthroat	18.04 lbs	1993	Omak Lake	Dan Beardslee
Westslope Cutthroat	1.44 lbs	2000	Half Moon Lake	John E. Moore
Dolly Varden	10 lbs 15 oz	1999	Whitechuck River	Leroy Thompson

COLD WATER RECORDS (cont.) Washington Game Fish Records - Updated April 30, 2002

Species	Weight	Year	Where	Angler
Golden Trout	3.81 lbs	1991	Unnamed water	Mark S. Morris
Lake Trout	35.44 lbs	2001	Lake Chelan	John G. Hossack
Rainbow Trout	25.71 lbs	2002	Rufus Woods Lake	Dick Hill
Beardslee Rainbow	16 lbs 5 oz	1989	Lake Crescent	Richard L. Bates
Summer Steelhead	35 lbs 1 oz	1973	Snake River	Gilbert Pierson
Winter Steelhead	32 lbs 12 oz	1980	East Fork Lewis	Gene Maygra
Kokanee	5.47 lbs	1993	Lake Roosevelt	Don Growt
Chinook Salmon	68.26 lbs	1992	Elochoman River	Mark Salmon
Chum Salmon	27.97 lbs	1997	Satsop River	Johnny Wilson
Coho Salmon	25.27 lbs	2001	Quinault River	Brad Wilson
Pink Salmon	14.86 lbs	2001	Skykomish River	Alex Minerich
Sockeye Salmon	10 lbs 10 oz	1982	Lake Washington	Gary Krasselt
Shad	3.44 lbs	1999	Columbia River	Pete Green
Grayling	No state record, season closed			
Lake Whitefish	6.63 lbs	1997	Lake Roosevelt	Jerry Hamilton
Mountain Whitefish	5 lbs 2 oz	1983	Columbia River	Steven Becken
Mountain Sucker	No state record			

WARM WATER RECORDS Washington Game Fish Records - Updated April 30, 2002

Species	Weight	Year	Where	Angler
Largemouth Bass	11 lbs 9 oz	1977	Banks Lake	Carl Pruitt
Smallmouth Bass	8 lbs 12 oz	1966	Columbia River	Ray Wonacott
Burbot	17.01 lbs	1993	Palmer Lake	Patrick Bloomer
Carp	41 lbs 4 oz	1980	Long Lake	Kevin Wolf
Brown Bullhead Catfish	11 lbs 5/8 oz	2000	Unnamed lake	Justin E. Andrews
Black Bullhead Catfish	1.75 lbs	1998	Mud Lake	John E. Moore
Yellow Bullhead	1.63 lbs	1994	Banks Lake	Mike Schlueter
Blue Catfish	17 lbs 12 oz	1975	Columbia River	Rangle Hawthorne
Channel Catfish	36.20 lbs	1999	I-82 Pond #6	Ross Kincaid
Flathead Catfish	22.8 lbs	1981	Snake River	C.L. McCary
Black Crappie	4 lbs 8 oz	1956	Lake Washington	John W. Smart
White Crappie	2.8 lbs	1988	Burbank Slough	Don J. Benson
Yellow Perch	2 lbs 12 oz	1969	Snelson's Slough	Andrew Joe Wallman
Northern Pike	32.2 lbs	1995	Long Lake	Fred R. Ruetsch
Tiger Muskie	31.25 lbs	2001	Mayfield Lake	John V. Bays
Bridgelip Sucker	3.06 lbs	1999	Palmer Lake	Pete Green
Largescale Sucker	5.34 lbs	2001	Mason Lake	Andrew Joe Wallman
Longnose Sucker	No state record			
Northern Pikeminnow	7.36 lbs	2000	Mason Lake	Andrew Joe Wallman
Peamouth Chub	.99 lbs	1995	Hanford Reach	Silvia Sanchez
Bluegill Sunfish	2 lbs 5.3 oz	1984	Tampico Park Pond	Ron Hinote
Green Sunfish	.79 lbs	1994	Bailey Lake	Mickey Hough
Pumpkinseed Sunfish	12 oz	1977	Hicks Lake	Doug Molohon
Rock Bass	1 lbs 6 oz	1981	Steilacoom Lake	William Jackson
Warmouth	.53 lbs	1996	Silver Lake	Linda Hatlelid
Walleye	18.90 lbs	2002	Columbia River	Kimo Gabriel

TEACHING CHILDREN

Above: Benton Lewis cradles a big summer-run Deschutes River steelhead he caught on a spinner. Photo by Jon Lewis

Below: Jennifer Lewis with a big Crane Prairie rainbow. Note the chunk missing from the tail. Something bigger was down there. Photo by Gary Lewis

For her fourth birthday we gave my daughter Jennifer a fishing rod. Tiffany, our oldest, had been fishing with her own for several years already. The three of us spent a few hours over the next month and a half, practicing for the trout opener.

We went over the basics again and again. Pinch the line against the rod, flip the bail open, cast, reel, stop and wait. If you feel a tug on the line, then lift the rod quick and start reeling. We practiced this without hooks in the house, then later in the backyard.

On the morning the season opened, we bought a dozen worms and headed for the lake.

There were deer in the trail and we gave them time to get away from us before we headed down the path. The girls carry their own gear and I had to stop and wait while they maneuvered tackle boxes, snacks and bait along the trail.

The rods were rigged the night before. Fresh knots held hooks to leaders and weights were crimped to the line just above a barrel swivel. Above the weight, I fastened a cork which could be adjusted to coincide with the depth the fish were holding.

The water was clear but high from recent rain and I could see a large dark shadow on the bottom. The water had a slight current and so I cast upstream first to let Jen's bait drift into the shadow. I set the rod down and helped Tiff cast her bait.

The shadow moved beneath the bobbers and soon a fish was taking Jen's bait, the bobber dancing and weaving.

Now that was all well and good except that Jennifer wasn't paying attention. Four year-old fisherpersons are easily distracted. When I called, she came running but the fish and the worm were long gone. Next it was Tiff's turn and I took the liberty of setting the hook myself before calling her from her play. As she cranked in the first fish of the day I turned to see Jen's bobber going under. Soon there were two fish coming to the bank and a couple of little girls who were suddenly a lot more interested than they had been a few minutes ago.

With so many things competing for a child's attention, fishing, if it is to be appreciated, must be exciting for them. An older child may have the patience to sit and watch a cork or cast a fly for an hour without a strike but a younger one needs action. Consider the chances of catching fish before you make the trip. And think about leaving your own rod at home the first few times. This is their fishing trip, not yours.

The weather can change quickly early in the season so bring warm clothes and something to change into if someone falls in. Bring something to eat and drink as well. Allow children the freedom to play on the bank and spend a little time looking at the bugs that live under the rocks. Explain that the trout don't just eat worms, but that their diet consists mainly of insects. Make it interesting and fun.

Bring a camera so that you can preserve your catch and the fun on film. And when the whining starts, find a way to make them laugh and smile again. But get ready to leave. It's better to go home smiling so their memory of fishing is a positive one.

Start off with tackle matched to their size, but choose it carefully. A light five to six foot rod is about right for a three to four foot child. Don't skimp on the rod or reel. A good reel will help keep tangles to a minimum. A bad reel will go a long way toward making everybody miserable.

Fill the reel with good line. The better lines won't tangle as easily and resist abrasions that could cause the line to break just when a trout is being banked. Four-to-six pound test is perfect for trout. It casts easier than heavier line and won't spook as many fish. Put a few barrel swivels in with their tackle. You will tie a swivel on the end of the main line and then tie a twenty inch leader on the end of that. Knot a No. 10 or 12 bait hook to the leader. Buy hooks with a non-reflective finish and barbs to hold the bait. I stay away from the snelled hooks because of the short leader length, heavy line and large hooks that spook trout. Kids need all the help they can get.

For bait fishing, it doesn't get much better than worms but you will do well to experiment with some of the other trout baits. Sometimes one bait or combination of baits will work when nothing else does.

Some people will want to encourage their children toward fly fishing. An easy way is to start with spin fishing tackle, bobber and bait then transition to

Above: Tegan Winters with a steelhead he caught on the North Fork Lewis. Photo courtesy Trisha Winters

bobber and fly on spin tackle. After a few fish have been caught this way then traditional fly tackle can be picked up.

With a little patience and preparation, even parents who aren't fishermen can teach and enjoy fishing with their children.

They may not remember everything you tell them the first time but these are days they'll recall in later years. This is part of what they'll remember about you. This is the time when you can show them the responsibilities of the outdoorsman and, more importantly, the responsibilities of growing up.

When the lessons are long, they get bored. Be prepared to end the interaction when the young mind wanders. End it on a positive note every time. Tell them how good they did and how much fun you had. This keeps the door open for next time.

Remember, when introducing a child to this or any sport, that your patience and understanding are the keys to their satisfaction and enjoyment. Teach them the elements of proper form, but most importantly, go slow and let them have fun learning.

Not only are you ensuring that you'll have someone to go fishing with, you're ensuring that the next generation will appreciate and enjoy the outdoors as much as you have.

GALLERY

Clockwise From Left: Deschutes River chinook salmon. Photo courtesy Gene Adams

Bob Pengra with a red-ear sunfish from Reynold's Pond. Photo courtesy Bob Pengra, Deschutes River Outfitters

Wade Stone with a Columbia River walleye. Photo by Gary Lewis

From Top: Peter Bowers with Deschutes River steelhead. Photo courtesy The Patient Angler

Lake trout. Gary Lewis Photo

John Garrison with a nice brown trout. Photo courtesy Garrison's Guide Service

INDEX OF ADVERTISERS

$18.95

46

7 39386 10703

© Copyright 2003

Gary Lewis Outdoors

P.O. Box 1364
Bend, Oregon 97709
www.garylewisoutdoors.com

ISBN 0-971410-07-0

51895

9 780971 410077